Everybody's
Favorite
Series No. 16

Trade Mark

GILBERT AND SULLIVAN

FOREWORD *In the world of music, whenever perfect welding of lyrics and music is discussed and commented upon, highest praise is unfailingly given to the works of W. S. Gilbert and Sir Arthur Sullivan.*

The constant revivals of the Gilbert and Sullivan operettas by professional and amateur groups are definite proof that the years have not dulled one whit, the brilliance of the lyrics or the absolute perfection of the music.

The collection which we offer in this volume includes not only the outstanding songs from the most famous of the operettas but also the story of each opera and a description of the action. Consequently, the songs take on a new significance when their place in the continuity of the opera is indicated.

To the millions of music lovers to whom the works of Gilbert and Sullivan represent a never-ending source of enjoyment, we respectfully dedicate this volume.

THE PUBLISHER

Order No. AM 40114
International Standard Book Number: 0.8256.2016.3

Exclusive Distributors:
Music Sales Corporation, 225 Park Avenue South, New York, NY 10003
Music Sales Limited, 8/9 Frith Street, London W1V 5TZ England
Music Sales Pty. Limited, 120 Rothschild Street, Rosebery, Sydney, NSW 2018, Australia

Printed in the United States of America by
Vicks Lithograph and Printing Corporation

EVERYBODY'S FAVORITE
GILBERT AND SULLIVAN ALBUM

CONTENTS

THE GONDOLIERS — 121

Dance A Cachucha — 136
Enterprise Of Martial Kind — 125
I Am A Courtier — 142
I Stole The Prince — 130
One Of Us Will Be A Queen — 134
There Lived a King — 139
There Was A Time — 127
We're Called Gondolieri — 121
When A Merry Maiden Marries — 132
Finale — 145

IOLANTHE — 73

Fal Lal Lal — 88
Good Morrow, Good Lover — 76
He Loves — 93
March Of The Peers — 81
None Shall Part Us — 78
Oh! Foolish Fay — 91
Said I To Myself, Said I — 86
The Law — 84
We Are Dainty Little Fairies — 73
Finale — 95

THE MIKADO — 4

A Wandering Minstrel — 4
Braid The Raven Hair — 25
Entrance Of The Mikado — 31
Flowers That Bloom In The Spring — 33
He's Going To Marry Yum Yum — 23
Here's A Howdy-do — 28
I've Got A Little List — 13
Taken From The County Jail — 11
The Moon And I — 26
The Lord High Executioner — 10
Three Little Maids From School — 16
There Is Beauty — 36
Tit Willow — 35
Were You Not To Koko Plighted — 20
Finale — 40

PATIENCE — 148

I Cannot Tell — 148
If You Want A Receipt — 151
Love Is A Plaintive Song — 161
Magnet In A Hardware Shop — 159
Prithee, Pretty Maiden — 155
Silvered Is The Raven Hair — 157
When I Go Out Of Door — 164
Finale — 166

H.M.S. PINAFORE — 42

Carefully On Tiptoe Stealing — 67
Farewell My Own — 69
I Am The Captain Of The Pinafore — 48
I'm Called Little Butter-cup — 45
Monarch Of The Sea — 53
Never Mind The Why Or Wherefore — 64
Refrain Audacious Tar — 59
Sorry Her Lot — 51
Things Are Seldom What They Seem — 61
We Sail The Ocean Blue — 42
When I Was A Lad — 56
Finale — 72

THE PIRATES OF PENZANCE — 97

Climbing Over Rocky Mountain — 100
For Some Ridiculous Reason — 114
I Am The Very Model — 108
Oh, Better Far To Live And Die — 97
Oh, Is There Not One Maiden — 102
Oh, Leave Me Not To Pine — 115
Pirate Chorus — 118
Policemen's Chorus — 112
Poor Wandering One — 104
When A Felon's Not Engaged — 116

TRIAL BY JURY — 168

All The Legal Furies Seize You — 182
Comes The Broken Flower — 175
Edwin Sued By Angelina — 168
I Love Him — 181
When First My Old, Old Love I Knew — 171
When I Was Called To The Bar — 173
With A Sense Of Deep Emotion — 178

YEOMEN OF THE GUARD — 185

A Private Buffoon — 201
A Man Who Would Woo — 205
Funeral March — 200
I Have A Song — 192
Is Life A Boon — 189
Strange Adventure — 203
Though Tear And Long-Drawn Sigh — 198
When A Maiden Loves — 185
When Our Gallant Norman Foes — 187
Finale — 207

EVERYBODY'S FAVORITE
GILBERT AND SULLIVAN ALBUM

ALPHABETICAL CONTENTS

A

All The Legal Furies Seize You (Trial By Jury) 183

B

Braid The Raven Hair (The Mikado) 25

C

Carefully On Tiptoe Stealing (H.M.S. Pinafore) 67
Climbing Over Rocky Mountain
  (The Pirates Of Penzance)........................ 100
Comes The Broken Flower (Trial By Jury) 175

D

Dance A Cachucha (The Gondoliers)................. 136

E

Edwin Sued By Angelina (Trial By Jury) 168
Enterprise Of Martial Kind (The Gondoliers) 125
Entrance Of The Mikado (The Mikado) 31

F

Fa! La! La! (Iolanthe)...................................... 88
Farewell My Own (H.M.S. Pinafore) 69
Flowers That Bloom In The Spring (The Mikado) 33
For Some Ridiculous Reason
  (The Pirates Of Penzance) 114
Funeral March (Yeomen Of The Guard) 200

G

Gondoliers, The 121
Good Morrow, Good Lover (Iolanthe)................. 76

H

He Loves (Iolanthe) 93
Here's A Howdy-do (The Mikado)...................... 28
He's Going To Marry Yum Yum (The Mikado) .. 23

I

I Am A Courtier (The Gondoliers) 142
I Am The Captain Of The Pinafore
  (H.M.S. Pinafore) 48
I Am The Very Model (The Pirates Of Penzance) 108
I Cannot Tell (Patience) 148
I Have A Song (Yeomen Of The Guard) 192
I Love Him (Trial By Jury)................................ 181
I Stole The Prince (The Gondoliers) 130
If You Want A Receipt (Patience) 151
I'm Called Little Butter-cup (H.M.S. Pinafore) 45
Iolanthe 73
Is Life A Boon (Yeomen Of The Guard) 189
I've Got A Little List (The Mikado) 13

L

Law, The (Iolanthe) 84
Lord High Executioner, The (The Mikado).......... 10
Love Is A Plaintive Song (Patience) 161

M

Magnet In A Hardware Shop (Patience) 159
Man Who Would Woo, A
  (Yeomen Of The Guard) 205
March Of The Peers (Iolanthe) 81
Mikado, The 4
Monarch Of The Sea (H.M.S. Pinafore) 53
Moon And I, The (The Mikado) 26

N

Never Mind The Why Or Wherefore
  (H.M.S. Pinafore) 64
None Shall Part Us (Iolanthe)........................... 78

O

Oh, Better Far To Live And Die
  (The Pirates Of Penzance) 97
Oh! Foolish Fay (Iolanthe)............................... 91
Oh! Is There Not One Maiden
  (The Pirates Of Penzance) 102
Oh, Leave Me Not To Pine
  (The Pirates Of Penzance) 115
One Of Us Will Be A Queen (The Gondoliers) .. 134

P

Patience 148
Pinafore, H. M. S. 42
Pirate Chorus (The Pirates Of Penzance) 118
Pirates Of Penzance, The 97
Policemen's Chorus (The Pirates Of Penzance) 112
Poor Wandering One (The Pirates Of Penzance) 104
Prithee Pretty Maiden (Patience)...................... 155
Private Buffoon, A (Yeomen Of The Guard) 201

R

Refrain Audacious Tar (H.M.S. Pinafore)............ 59

S

Said I To Myself, Said I (Iolanthe)..................... 86
Silvered Is The Raven Hair (Patience) 157
Sorry Her Lot (H.M.S. Pinafore)........................ 51
Strange Adventure (Yeomen Of The Guard) 203

T

Taken From The County Jail (The Mikado) 11
There Is Beauty (The Mikado) 36
There Lived A King (The Gondoliers) 139
There Was A Time (The Gondoliers) 127
Things Are Seldom What They Seem
  (H.M.S. Pinafore) 61
Three Little Maids From School (The Mikado) 16
Though Tear and Long-Drawn Sigh
  (Yeomen Of The Guard) 198
Tit Willow (The Mikado).................................. 35
Trial By Jury.. 168

W

Wandering Minstrel, A (The Mikado)................. 4
We Are Dainty Little Fairies (Iolanthe) 73
We Sail The Ocean Blue (H.M.S. Pinafore) 42
We're Called Gondolieri (The Gondoliers)........ 121
Were You Not To Koko Plighted (The Mikado) 20
When A Felon's Not Engaged
  (The Pirates Of Penzance) 116
When A Maiden Loves (Yeomen Of The Guard) 185
When A Merry Maiden Marries (The Gondoliers) 132
When First My Old, Old Love I Knew
  (Trial By Jury) 171
When I Go Out Of Door (Patience) 164
When I Was Called To The Bar (Trial By Jury) 173
When I Was A Lad (H.M.S. Pinafore) 56
With A Sense Of Deep Emotion (Trial By Jury) 178
When Our Gallant Norman Foes
  (Yeomen Of The Guard)............................. 187

Y

Yeomen Of The Guard.. 185

THE MIKADO
or
The Town Of Titipu

Libretto by
W. S. GILBERT

Music by
SIR ARTHUR SULLIVAN

Cast of Characters

The MIKADO of JAPAN
NANKI-POO, His son
KOKO, Lord High Executioner
POOH-BAH, Lord High Everything Else
PISH-TUSH, a noble Lord
YUM-YUM ⎫
PITTI-SING ⎬ Wards of Koko. "Three Little Maids from School"
PEEP-BO ⎭
KATISHA, an elderly spinster

Japan; about 1800

Act I

A group of nobles are assembled in the courtyard of Koko's palace when Nanki-Poo enters and inquires where Yum-Yum is to be found. He is disguised as a wandering minstrel, carrying a guitar and a number of songs. He has fled in this disguise from the wrath of his father, the Mikado, because he refused to marry Katisha, an elderly spinster.

A Wandering Minstrel
Nanki-Poo

NANKI-POO

Allegretto con grazia

A wand-'ring min-strel I, a thing of shreds__ and pat-ches, Of bal-lads songs and snat-ches, And dream-y lull-a-by!__ My cat-a-logue is long, through ev-'ry pas - sion rang-ing And to your hu-mors chang-ing I

tune my sup-ple song_____ I tune my sup - ple

song:_____ Are you in sen-ti-men-tal mood? I'll sigh with you, oh,_____

Andante espressivo

sor - row! On maid-en's cold-ness do you brood? I'll do so, too oh,_____

sor - row, sor - row! I'll charm your will-ing ears with songs of lov-ers fears,

While sym-pa-the-tic tears my cheeks be-dew oh, _____ sor-row, sor-row.

Allegro marziale

But if pa-tri-ot-ic sen-ti-ment is want-ed, I've pat-ri-o-tic bal-lads cut and dried; For wher-e'er our coun-try's ban-ner may be plant-ed, All oth-er lo-cal ban-ners are de-fied! Our war-ri-ors, in ser-ried ranks as-sem-bled, Nev-er

quail, or they con-ceal it if they do, And I should-n't be sur-prised if na-tions

trem-bled be-fore the might-y troops, the troops of Ti - ti - pu! We should-n't be sur-prised if

na-tions trem-bled, trem-bled with a-larm be-fore the might-y troops the troops of Ti - ti -

MEN

NANKI-FOO

pu! **Allegro non troppo** And if you call for a song of the sea, We'll

heave the cap-stan 'round, With a yo heave ho, for the wind is _ free, Her

an-chor's a-trip and her helm's a-lee, Hur-rah for the home-ward bound! Yo ho— heave

MEN

ho Hur-rah for the home-ward bound! To lay a-loft in a howl-ing breeze may

NANKI-POO

tick-le a lands-man's taste, But the hap-piest hour a sail-or sees is when he's down at an

in-land town with his Nan-cy on his knees Yo Ho! And his arm a-round her waist Then

MEN

man the cap-stan off we go, As the fid-dler swings us 'round, With a Yo Heave Ho, and a

9

Nanki-Poo tells the noblemen he has heard that Koko, to whom Yum-Yum is betrothed, has been sentenced to be decapitated under the Mikado's decree against flirting and that he hopes to persuade Yum-Yum to hear his suit. Pish-Tush informs him that Koko has been reprieved and has now been promoted to the exalted rank of Lord High Executioner. At this time Pooh-Bah enters and explains that, as all the public officers of Titipu had quit their posts because Koko, a humble plebian tailor, had been made Lord High Executioner, he Pooh-Bah, had condescended to accept all the vacancies and, incidentally, all their salaries. Nanki-Poo asks how it is that the great Lord High Everything Else is so condescending as to talk to him, a humble minstrel, and Pooh-Bah tells him that he likes to mortify his pride by being democratic with persons of low degree. Pooh-Bah also tells him that he "retails state secrets at a low figure" and any further information concerning Yum-Yum will come under the head of a "state secret." Nanki-Poo gives him money and Pooh-Bah informs him that Koko is to wed Yum-Yum that same day. He advises Nanki-Poo to resign himself to the fact that his suit is hopeless. At this point the Lord High Executioner himself enters.

The Lord High Executioner
Chorus

fer, To the no-ble Lord, to the no-ble Lord, to the Lord High Ex - e - cu-tion-er!

Taken From the County Jail
Koko

Tak-en from the coun-ty jail, By a set of cur-ious chan-ces, Lib-er-a-ted then on bail, On my own re-cog-ni-zan-ces; Waft-ed by a fav-'ring gale, As one some-times is in tran-ces,

To a height that few can scale, Save by long and wea-ry dan-ces; Sure-ly nev-er had a

male Un-der such like cir-cum-stan-ces, So ad-ven-tur-ous a tale Which may

rank with most ro-man-ces. Tak-en from the coun-ty jail By a set of cur-ious

p stacc.

chan-ces, Sure-ly nev-er had a male so ad-ven-tur-ous a tale.

Koko thanks the people for their reception and reveals his future plans as Lord High Executioner in the following "list."

I've Got A Little List
Koko and Chorus of Men

Allegretto

mf

As

some day it may hap-pen that a vic-tim may be found, I've got a lit-tle list, I've
nig-ger ser-e-na-der and the oth-ers of his race, And the pia-no or-gan-ist, I've
Ni-si-Pri-us nui-sance, who just now is rath-er rife, The ju-di-cial hu-mor-ist, I've

got a lit-tle list, Of so-ci-e-ty of-fen-ders who might
got him on the list! And the peo-ple who eat pep-per-mint and
got him on the list! All fun-ny fel-lows, com-ic men, and

well be un-der-ground, And who ne-ver would be missed, who ne-ver would be missed! There's the
puff it in your face, They ne-ver would be missed, they ne-ver would be missed! Then the
clowns of pri-vate life, They'd none of them be missed, they'd none of them be missed! And a -

pest - i - len - tial nui - san - ces who write for au - to - graphs, All
i - di - ot who prais - es with en - thu - si - as - tic tone, All
pol - o - get - ic states - men of the com - pro - mis - ing kind, Such as

peo - ple who have flab - by hands and ir - ri - tat - ing laughs All
cen - tu - ries but this and ev - 'ry coun - try but his own; And the
"What - d'ye - call - him" "Thing - em - bob" and like - wise "Nev - er mind", And

child-ren who are up in dates, and floor you with 'em flat, All per-sons who in shak-ing hands, shake
la - dy from the pro-vin-ces, who dress-es like a guy, And who does-n't think she dan-ces but would
"'St - 'st-'st" and "What's-his-name", and al - so "You know who" The task of fill-ing up the blanks I'd

hands with you like that.   And   all third per-sons who on spoil-ing tete-a-tetes in-sist,   They'd
rath - er   like   to try. And that   sin-gu - lar an - o - ma -ly,   the la - dy no - ve-list,   I
rath - er   leave   to you. But   it   real-ly does-n't mat-ter whom you put up on the list, For they'd

CHORUS

none   of them be missed, they'd none of them be missed!   He's   got 'em on the list,   He's
don't think she'd be missed, I'm *sure* she'd not be missed!   He's   got her on the list,   He's
none   of them be missed, they'd none of them be missed! You may put 'em on the list, You may

got 'em   on   the list; And they'll none of   'em be missed,   they'll none of   'em be
got her   on   the list; And I   don't think she'll be missed,   I'm *sure* she'll not be
put 'em   on   the list, And they'll none of   'em be missed,   they'll none of 'em be

1   *KOKO*   **2**

missed!
missed!   There's the
     And   that missed!

f

Koko talks with Pooh-Bah of his plans for his marriage. Yum-Yum now enters with Peep-Bo and Pitti-Sing, the "three little maids from school."

Three Little Maids From School

Yum Yum, Pitti Sing, Peep-Bo and Chorus

PITTI-SING

Life is a joke that's just be-gun!

ALL ... *ALL*

Three lit-tle maids from school. ... Three lit-tle maids, who

all un-war- y, Come from a la-dies sem-i-na-ry, Freed from its ge-nius tu-te-la-ry

Three lit-tle maids from school, three lit-tle maids from school.

YUM-YUM   *PEEP-BO*   *PITTI-SING*

One lit-tle maid is a bride Yum Yum, Two lit-tle maids in at-ten-dance come. Three lit-tle maids is the

ALL   *YUM-YUM*

to-tal sum, Three lit-tle maids from school!   From

PEEP-BO   *PITTI-SING*

three lit-tle maids take one a-way Two lit-tle maids re-main and they, Won't have to wait ve-ry

The three little maids recognize Nanki-Poo as the second trombone player in the Titipu band (another disguise) and present him to Koko. Nanki-Poo frankly tells Koko that he loves his ward, Yum-Yum, but Koko is not disturbed and assures Nanki-Poo he is flattered by the substantiation of his own judgment as he loves Yum-Yum himself. When Yum-Yum and Nanki-Poo are left alone he reveals to her that he is really the son of the Mikado. They proceed to demonstrate to each other the kisses and caresses in which they would indulge if Yum-Yum were not betrothed to Koko.

Were You Not To Koko Plighted

Yum Yum and Nanki Poo

As Nanki-Poo and Yum-Yum leave, Koko rushes in with a letter from the Mikado, in which it is decreed that unless Koko executes someone within a month, he will be discharged as Lord High Executioner. Pooh-Bah suggests that Koko execute himself as he is already under indictment but Koko rejects this as extremely awkward and almost impossible. As they are casting about for some one to execute, Nanki-Poo enters with a rope, bent on committing suicide over his hopeless love for Yum-Yum. Pooh-Bah and Koko dissuade him from this pointing out that if he must die, why not do it in style at a public execution with bands playing, flags flying, a grand parade, girls crying, bells tolling, etc. Nanki-Poo agrees to die in a month if he may marry Yum-Yum immediately and live with her until the execution. This satisfies Koko and the marriage arrangements are made.

He's Going To Marry Yum-Yum!

Pitti-Sing and Chorus

For he's go-ing to mar-ry Yum Yum (Yum Yum) Your an-ger pray bur-y, for all will be mer-ry, I

think you had bet-ter suc-cumb (cumb cumb) And join our ex-press-ions of glee, On this

sub-ject I pray you be dumb (dumb dumb) You'll find there are ma-ny who'll wed for a pen-ny The

word for your guid-ance is "mum"(mum mum) There's lots of good fish in the sea! On this

sub-ject we pray you be dumb, dumb, dumb. We think you had bet-ter suc-cumb, cumb, cumb! You'll find there are

ma-ny who'll wed for a pen-ny, who'll wed for a pen-ny, There are lots of good fish in the sea! There are

lots of good fish in the sea! There's lots of good fish, good fish in the sea! There's lots of good

fish, good fish in the sea, in the sea, in the sea, in the sea, in the sea.___

Act II

Yum-Yum with Peep-Bo and Pitti-Sing and a bevy of girls are discovered in Koko's garden preparing for her wedding.

Braid the Raven Hair
Chorus of Girls

Braid the ra - ven hair, weave the sup - ple tress_ Deck the mai - den fair_ in her love - li - ness. Paint the pret - ty face, dye the co - ral lip Em - pha-size the grace of her la - dy - ship! Art and na - ture thus al -

Copyright MCMXXXVIII—by Amsco Music Publishing Co.

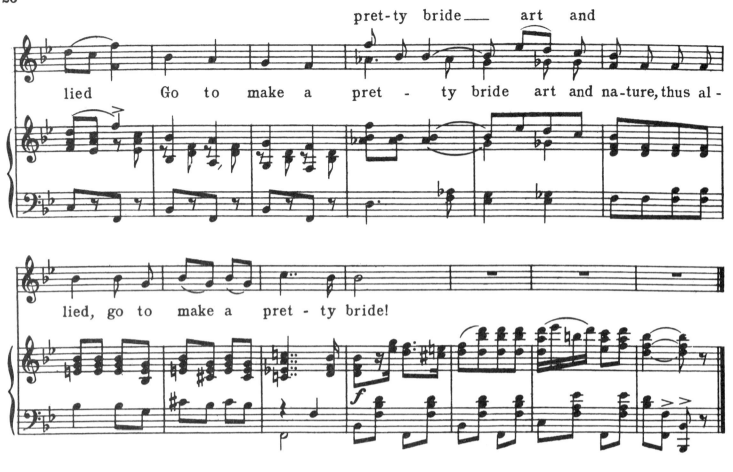

pret-ty bride___ art and

lied Go to make a pret - ty bride art and na-ture, thus al-

lied, go to make a pret - ty bride!

The Moon and I

Yum - Yum

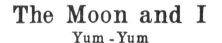

Andante comodo

The sun, whose rays are all a-blaze with ev - er
Oh, serve his flame, that pla-cid dame, the moon's ce -

liv - ing glo - ry,   Does not de - ny his ma - jes - ty, he scorns to tell a sto - ry!
les-tial high-ness;   There's not a trace up - on her face of dif - fi-dence or shy - ness:

The girls thoughtfully remind Yum-Yum that her happiness with Nanki-Poo will only be for one month and she is in tears when Nanki-Poo enters with Pish-Tush. They are vainly trying to comfort her when Koko arrives with the unhappy information that the Japanese Law demands that when a married man is executed his wife must buried with him.

Here's A Howdy Do

Yum-Yum, Nanki Poo and Koko

YUM-YUM
Here's a how-de-do!

Allegro

If I mar-ry you, When your time has come to per-ish, Then the maid-en whom you cher-ish

Must be slaugh-ter'd too! Here's a how-de-do! Here's a how-de-do!

NANKI POO
Here's a pret-ty mess! In a month or

cresc.

less,   I must die with-out a wed-ding! Let the bit-ter tears I'm shed-ding wit-ness my dis-

tress   Here's a pret - ty mess!   Here's a pret - ty mess!

KOKO

Here's a state of things!   To her life she clings!   Mat-ri-mo-ni - al de-vo-tion

Does-n't seem to suit her no-tion, bur-i - al it brings!   Here's a state of things!

ALL
(Yum-Yum on Melody)

Here's a state of things! With a pas-sion that's in-tense I wor-ship You

and_ a - dore, But the laws of com-mon sense we ought-n't to_ ig - nore. If
(You)

what he says is true, 'Tis death to mar-ry you! Here's a pret-ty state of things!
(I say)

Here's a pret-ty how-de-do! Here's a pret-ty state of things, a pret-ty state of

things! Here's a pret-ty, pret-ty state of things!

SPOKEN

Here's a pretty how-de-do!

While they are still trying to figure a way out of the dilemma, Pooh-Bah arrives with the news that the Mikado himself is coming to see if his orders have been obeyed. Koko in desperation demands that Nanki Poo allow himself to be executed at once. Nanki Poo agrees but Koko's heart fails him and they draw up a false paper showing that the execution has taken place. The procession heralding the Mikado enters.

Entrance Of Mikado
Chorus

Moderato

The Mikado enters with Katisha, his self styled "daughter-in-law-elect." Koko tells him that the execution has taken place according to his orders. The Mikado then tells Koko that he also came to Titipu to search for his son who has been masquerading under the name of Nanki Poo as a wandering minstrel. Then, to everyone's horror and dismay, Katisha, reading the death certificate announces that it is Nanki Poo the missing son, who has been executed. Koko is distracted and begs the Mikado's forgiveness. The Mikado graciously forgives him but reminds Koko that there is a law covering the killing of the heir apparent which demands the punishment of being boiled in oil or "something equally unpleasant." Koko frantically tries to persuade Nanki Poo to come back to life. Nanki Poo finally agrees to this on condition that Koko marry Katisha and leave Nanki Poo himself free to marry Yum Yum.

The Flowers That Bloom In The Spring

Nanki-Poo and Koko
Yum-Yum, Pitti-Sing and Pooh-Bah

rall.

that's what we mean when we say that a thing is wel-come as flowers that bloom in the spring. Tra
that's what I mean when I say, or I sing "O both-er the flowers that bloom in the spring." Tra

rall.

ALL
f

la la la la, tra la la la la, The flow-ers that bloom in the spring. Tra
la la la la, tra la la la la, O, both-er the flow-ers of spring. Tra

la la la·la, tra la la la la, tra la la la la la. là.
la la la la, tra la la la la, tra la la la la la

Pursuant to his agreement with Nanki Poo, Koko immediately proceeds to make violent love to Katisha and tells her he will surely die a suicide if she refuses to marry him. He cites a case where even a little bird will die of unrequited love.

Tit-Willow
Koko

On a tree by a riv-er a
He slapped at his chest as he
Now I feel just as sure as I'm

lit-tle tom-tit sang "wil-low, tit wil-low, tit wil-low." And I
sat on the bough, sing-ing "wil-low, tit wil-low, tit wil-low." And a
sure that my name is-n't "wil-low, tit wil-low, tit wil-low." That 'twas

said to him Dick-ie bird, why do you sit, sing-ing wil-low, tit wil-low, tit
cold per-spir-a-tion be-span-gled his brow, oh— wil-low, tit wil-low, tit
blight-ed af-fec-tion that made him ex-claim, oh,— wil-low, tit wil-low, tit

wil - low? "Is it weak - ness of in - tell - ect, bird - ie?" I cried "Or a
wil - low! He_ sobbed and he sighed, and a gur - gle he gave, Then he
wil - low! And if you re - main cal - lous and ob - du - rate, I shall_

rath - er tough worm in your lit - tle in - side?" With a shake of his poor lit - tle
plunged him - self in - to the bil - low - y wave, And an ech - o a - rose from the
per - ish as he did and you will know why, Though I prob - ab - ly shall not ex -

head he re - plied, "Oh wil - low, tit wil - low, tit wil - low!" wil - low!" wil - low!"
su - i - cide's grave "Oh wil - low, tit wil - low, tit
claim as I die, "Oh wil - low, tit wil - low, tit

Katisha is very much impressed with this sad tale and agrees to marry Koko. She tells Koko that although her face may not be beautiful she has a left shoulder blade that connoisseurs of beauty come
miles to see.

There Is Beauty In The Bellow Of The Blast
Koko and Katisha

Allegretto con brio

beau - ty in the bel-low of the blast, There is grand-eur in the growl-ing of the gale, There is el - o-quent out-pour-ing when the li - on is a-roar-ing, And the ti - ger is a-lash-ing of his tail. Yes, I like to see a ti - ger from the Con - go or the Ni - ger, And es - pe - cial - ly when lash-ing of his

The Mikado now demands the execution of all the persons involved in the death of Nanki Poo. Katisha begs for mercy and tells the Mikado she has married Koko. Nanki Poo appears and Koko hastens to explain that as Nanki Poo was condemned by the Mikado's law, he was legally dead and practically dead, so why not say he really was dead? The Mikado appears to be satisfied and the opera ends with everybody happy.

Finale
Ensemble

cheer, Joy - ous, ioy - ous

shout! With laugh-ing song and mer-ry dance, With laugh-ing song and mer-ry

dance, With song _____ and

dance.

H. M. S. PINAFORE
or
"The Lass That Loved A Sailor"

Libretto by:
W. S. GILBERT

Music by:
SIR ARTHUR SULLIVAN

Cast of Characters

SIR JOSEPH PORTER . . . . First Lord of the Admiralty.
CAPTAIN CORCORAN. . . . . Captain of Her Majesty's Ship "Pinafore."
JOSEPHINE . . . . his daughter.
LITTLE BUTTERCUP . . . . a peddler.
RALPH RACKSTRAW. . . . . a sailor in love with Josephine.
DICK DEADEYE. . . . . a sailor.
HEBE . . . . one of Sir Joseph's cousins.
Chorus of Sir Joseph's relatives, sailors, marines, etc.

Act I

SCENE — The deck of H. M. S. Pinafore, at anchor in the bay of Portsmouth, England, about 1880. Sailors are busy cleaning the deck, splicing rope, polishing brass, etc., while singing the opening number.

We Sail the Ocean Blue
OPENING CHORUS
Chorus of Sailors

Allegretto pesante

We sail the o-cean blue, And our sau-cy ship's a beau-ty; We're

so-ber men and true, And at-ten-tive to our du-ty; When the

balls whis-tle free o'er the bright blue sea We stand to our guns all day, When at

an-chor we ride on the Ports-mouth tide, We've plen-ty of time for play, a-hoy! a-

hoy! The balls whis-tle free, a-hoy, a-hoy, The balls whis-tle free, we stand to our

guns, to our guns all day _____ We sail the o-cean

blue, And our sau-cy ships a beau-ty, We're so-ber men and true, And at-

ten-tive to our du-ty. Our sau-cy ship's a beau-ty, We're at-ten-tive to our

du-ty, We're so-ber men and true, we sail the o - - cean

blue.

rall.

"Little" Buttercup whose size is just the opposite of her name, comes aboard the ship to peddle all sorts of trinkets, knick-knacks, tobacco and delicacies to the sailors.

I'm Called Little Buttercup
Buttercup

snuff and to - bac - cy, And ex - cel - lent Jack - y; I've scis - sors and watch - es, and

knives, _____ I've rib - bons and la - ces to set off the fa - ces Of

pret - ty young sweet - hearts and wives. _____ I've trea - cle and tof - fee, I've

tea and I've cof - fee, Soft tom - my and suc - cu - lent chops, _____ I've

chick-ens and co-nies, and pret-ty po-lo-nies, And ex-cel-lent pep-per-mint drops. ___ Then buy of your But-ter-cup, Dear lit-tle But-ter-cup,

Sail-ors should nev-er be shy ___ So buy of your But-ter-cup,

Poor lit-tle But-ter-cup, Come! Of your But-ter-cup buy. ___

Buttercup confides that, although she looks the picture of health and happiness, she is consumed with a secret worry. She is interrupted by the entrance of Dick Deadeye whose baleful countenance with one "dead eye" causes a stir. Ralph Rackstraw also enters and tells them he is hopelessly in love with a lady far above his station. After some persuasion he confesses it is Josephine, the Captain's daughter whom he loves. At this point Captain Corcoran himself enters.

I Am the Captain of the Pinafore

Captain Corcoran and Chorus of Men

am the Cap-tain of the "Pin-a-fore" And a right good cap-tain too!
do my best to sat-is-fy you all__ And with you we're quite con-

You're__ ve-ry, ve-ry good and__ be it un-der-stood, I com-
tent! You're ex-ceed-ing-ly po-lite, and I think it on-ly right, To re-

mand a__ right good crew. We're__ ve-ry, ve-ry good and__
turn the__ com-pli-ment. We're ex-ceed-ing ly po-lite, and he

be it un-der-stood, He com-mands a_ right good crew. Tho' re-
thinks it on-ly right, To re-turn the_ com-pli - ment. Bad_

lat-ed to a peer, I can hand a reef and steer, Or ship_ a_ sel-va-
lan-guage or a-buse, I_ nev-er, nev-er use, What-ev-er the e-mer-gen_

gee; I am nev-er known to quail at the fu-ry of the gale, And I'm
cy; Though "both-er it" I may oc - ca-sion-al-ly say, I_

nev-er, nev-er sick at sea! What nev-er? No, nev-er, What
nev-er use a big, big D! What nev-er? No, nev-er, What

nev-er? Hard-ly ev-er! He's hard-ly ev-er sick at
nev-er? Hard-ly ev-er! Hard-ly ev-er swear a big, big

sea.
D! Then give three cheers and one cheer more For the har-dy Cap-tain of the

"Pin-a-fore," Then give three cheers and one cheer more For the Cap-tain of the "Pin-a-

fore."

I

After this song, the Captain and Buttercup are left alone on the deck. He confides to her that Sir Joseph Porter, the distinguished Lord of the Admiralty, wishes to marry his daughter, but Josephine does not seem to relish the idea. Buttercup sympathizes with the Captain and leaves. Josephine now makes her first appearance.

Sorry Her Lot, Who Loves Too Well

Josephine

Un poco animato

Hea - vy the sor - row that bows ___ the head When

cresc. love is a - live ___ and hope ___ is dead! When

love is a-live and hope ___ is dead. Sad is the

colla voce

love ___ is a - live, and hope ___ is dead. ___

The Captain asks Josephine why she does not encourage the attentions of Sir Joseph and she finally admits that she is in love with an ordinary sailor on her father's ship. However, after he pleads with her, she agrees to renounce the love so far beneath her station and encourage the suit of the great and distinguished Sir Joseph Porter. Just then, the coming of Sir Joseph is announced and he boards the ship accompanied by a crowd of his "sisters and his cousins and his aunts."

Monarch of the Sea
Sir Joseph Porter and Chorus

SIR JOSEPH

When at an-chor here I ride, My bo-som swells with pride, And I snap my fin-gers at a foe-man's taunts

HEBE

And so do his sis-ters and his cou-sins and his aunts,

CHOS.

And so do his sis-ters and his cou-sins and his aunts, His sis-ters and his cou-sins and his aunts.

SIR JOSEPH

But when the breez-es

blow, I gen-er-al-ly go be-low, And seek the se-clu-sion that a

HEBE

CHOS.

ca-bin grants. And so do his sis-ters and his cou-sins and his aunts, And so do his sis-ters and his

ALL

cou-sins and his aunts, And so do his sis-ters and his cou-sins and his aunts, His

sis-ters and his cou-sins, Whom he reck-ons by the doz-ens, and his aunts. _____

Sir Joseph outlines his rise to power in another song and tells them how they can "all be rulers of the Queen's Navee."

When I Was a Lad
Sir Joseph and Chorus

Allegro non troppo

When   I   was   a   lad   I
As   of - fice   boy   I   I
In   serv - ing   writs   I   I
Of   le - gal   knowl - edge   I   ac -
I   grew   so   rich   that
Now   lands - men   all,   who

served   a   term   As   of-fice boy   to   an at - tor - neys firm.   I
made   such   a mark That   they gave me the   post   of   a   Jun - ior clerk.   I
made   such   a name That   an ar - ti-cled   clerk   I   soon   be - came.   I
quired   such   a grip That they took   me   in - to the part - ner-ship, And that
I   was   sent By   a pock-et bo - rough in-to par - lia - ment.   I
ev - er   you may be,   If   you want   to   rise   to the top   of the tree,   If your

cleaned the win-dows and I swept the floor And I pol-ished up the han-dle of the
served the writs with a smile so bland And I cop-ied all the let-ters in a
wore clean col-lars and a bran' new suit For the pass ex-am-in-a-tion at the
Jun-ior part-ner-ship I ween Was the on-ly ship that I
al-ways vot-ed at my par-ty's call, And I nev-er tho't of think-ing for my-
soul isn't fet-tered to an of-fice stool, Be care-ful to be guid-ed by this

CHOS.

big front door. He — pol-ished up the han-dle of the
big round hand. He — cop-ied all the let-ters in a
in-sti-tute. For the pass ex-am-in-a-tion at the
ev-er had seen. Was the on-ly ship he
self at all. He — nev-er tho't of think-ing for him-
gold-en rule. Be — care-ful to be guid-ed by this

SIR JOSEPH

big — front door. I pol-ished up that han-dle so —
big — round hand. I cop-ied all the let-ters in a
in-sti-tute, That pass ex-am-in-a-tion did so
ev-er had seen. But that — kind of ship — so —
self — at all. I tho't — so lit-tle they re-
gold-en rule. Stick close — to your desks — and —

Sir Joseph inspects the crew, asks them how they are treated, and tells the Captain not to patronize the sailors too much because they are the equals of anyone else (except Sir Joseph). He is pleased with Ralph, whom he has singled out and presents him with a song to memorize, the text of which is "Love Levels All Ranks." The Captain and Sir Joseph retire to the cabin and the sailors to the lower deck. Josephine enters alone. Ralph resolves to tell her of his love before it is too late but she repulses his ardor.

Refrain, Audacious Tar!

Josephine and Ralph

Ralph calls all the sailors to the deck and draws a pistol to kill himself. Josephine is frightened and realizing the strength of Ralph's love for her, confesses that she really loves him too. The sailors are overjoyed, all except Dick Deadeye, and plan to take the happy couple ashore that very night and have a clergyman marry them. Dick Deadeye is against the plan but they are deaf to his warnings and the act closes with a gay nautical Chorus.

Act II

SCENE—The Same— At Night. The act opens with the Captain singing a sentimental song to the moon (while he accompanies himself on the mandolin). Buttercup is with him and he tells her although he is very fond of her, the difference in their stations forbids any sentimental intimacy. She seeks to prepare him for a change in the following number.

Things are Seldom What They Seem
Buttercup and Captain Corcoran

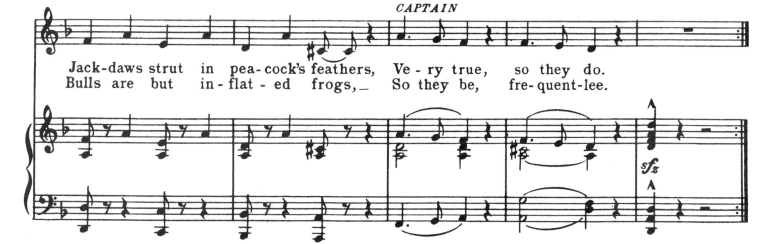

Things are sel - dom what they seem,
Black sheep dwell in ev - 'ry fold,

Skim milk mas - quer - ades as cream, High - lows pass as pat - ent leathers,
All that glit - ters is not gold, Storks turn out to be but logs,—

Jack-daws strut in pea-cock's feathers, Ve - ry true, so they do.
Bulls are but in - flat - ed frogs,— So they be, fre - quent-lee.

The meaning of this ditty is quite puzzling to the Captain but, before he can question Buttercup any further, Sir Joseph enters.   He is perturbed at Josephine's coldness toward his suit.   The Captain suggests that he remind her that "love levels all ranks."   Josephine enters and he again takes up his wooing, reminding her again that "love levels all ranks."   This really fortifies her determination to marry Ralph, but she appears to agree with Sir Joseph.

Never Mind the Why or Wherefore
Sir Joseph, the Captain and Josephine

SIR JOSEPH

Allegro vivace

Nev - er mind the why or where-fore, Love can lev - el ranks and there-fore I ad - mit the jur - is - dic - tion, Ab - ly have you played your part, You have car - ried firm con - vic - tion To my hes - i - ta - ting

SIR JOSEPH

JOSEPHINE

daugh-ter, And a Lord that rules the wa - ter, And a tar that ploughs the

ALL

ff

wa - ter. Let the air with joy be la - den

Rend with songs the air a - bove, For the un - ion of a maid - en

With the man who owns her love._____

The Captain's joy at the prospect of his daughter marrying a Lord of The Admiralty is short lived. Dick Deadeye mysteriously approaches him and tells him of her plan to elope and marry Ralph, the common sailor. The Captain conceals himself and the crew stealthily enter with Ralph, Josephine and Buttercup, intent on leaving the ship.

Carefully On Tip-toe Stealing
Chorus

Care-ful - ly on tip - toe
shore in fash - ion

steal - ing,   Breath-ing gent - ly   as   we   may,   Ev - 'ry
stead - y,   Hy - men will de - fray the fare,   For a

step with cau - tion feel - ing   We_ will soft ly creep a
cler - gy - man is rea - dy   To_ u - nite the hap - py

way.   Good-ness me!   Why what was that!   Sil - ent
pair.   Good-ness me!   Why what was that!   Sil - ent

The Captain angrily stops the party and demands an explanation. Sir Joseph appears on the scene just as the Captain in his rage has said "dam-me." Sir Joseph, shocked at such language by the Captain orders him to his cabin. He asks Ralph the reason for uncalled for profanity and Ralph explains that it was because the Captain caught him and Josephine in the act of eloping. At this explanation, Sir Joseph himself flies into a terrible rage and orders Ralph thrown in a dungeon.

Farewell, My Own

Ralph, Sir Joseph, Buttercup, Josephine and Chorus

dun - geon cell.____ A bone,____ a bone,____ I'll

pick with this sail - or fell, Let him be shown at once to his

dun - geon cell. He'll hear no tone__ of the maid-en he loves so

well! No tel - e-phone com-mun-i-cates with his cell!

Little Buttercup comes forward at this time with the most astonishing revelation of all. It seems that years ago she had run a "baby farm" and that when Captain Cocoran and Ralph were infants, she was their nurse and the two babies were accidentally "mixed up." In other words, the Captain should be Ralph and Ralph should be the Captain. So Ralph dons the Captain's uniform and the Captain dresses in Ralph's "common sailor" garb. Sir Joseph turns out to be not so keen on the saying "love levels all ranks" and decides to marry his cousin Hebe. The Captain devotes himself to little Buttercup, and Ralph and Josephine are at last free to enjoy their mutual happiness.

Finale
Ensemble

IOLANTHE
or
The Peer And The Peri

Libretto by
W. S. GILBERT

Music by
SIR ARTHUR SULLIVAN

Cast of Characters

STREPHON . . . . An Arcadian Shepherd
IOLANTHE . . . . A fairy, mother of Strephon
PHYLLIS . . . . An Arcadian Shepherdess also a ward in Chancery
PRIVATE WILLIS . . . . Of the Grenadier Guards
THE FAIRY QUEEN
THE LORD CHANCELLOR
CELIA ⎫
LEITA ⎬ FAIRIES
FLETA ⎭
Chorus of Peers, Fairies, etc.

The Scene is in Arcadia and England between 1700 and 1882

Act I

The opera opens in a beautiful forest in the fairyland known as Arcadia. The fairies, led by Celia, Leita and Fleta are dancing and singing.

We Are Dainty Little Fairies
Celia and Chorus of Fairies

CELIA

We are dain-ty lit-tle fair-ies, ev-er sing-ing, ev-er danc-ing. We in-dulge in our va-

ga-ries in a fash-ion most en-tranc-ing; If you ask the spec-ial

func-tion of our nev-er ceas-ing mo - tion, We re-ply with-out com-

CHORUS

punc-tion that we have-n't a-ny no-tion No! we have-n't a-ny no-tion! A - ny

no - tion! Trip-ping hi-ther, trip-ping thith-er, no-bo-dy knows why or whith-er, We must

dance, and we must sing, Round a - bout our fai - ry

ring. We are dain - ty lit - tle fai - ries, ev - er sing - ing, ev - er

danc - ing We in - dulge in our va - ga - ries in a fash - ion most en -

tranc - ing _____ most en - tranc - ing _____ most en -

Iolanthe, who has been banished for twenty-five years for marrying a mortal is brought before the queen and forgiven. She tells them that she has a son, 24 years old, half mortal and half fairy. He is a shepherd and in love with Phyllis, a shepherdess. Strephon, the son, then enters and tells Iolanthe that Phyllis is also a Ward in Chancery and that the Lord Chancellor has forbidden her to marry him. He feels that being half fairy is a detriment, but he is determined to marry her at any cost. The Queen of the Fairies then tells Strephon that she will help him to marry Phyllis, all in proper time. The fairies leave and Phyllis herself enters, dancing and singing and playing the flageolet.

Good Morrow, Good Lover
Phyllis and Strephon

Strephon urges her to marry at once but she reminds him that should they marry without the consent of the Lord Chancellor it would mean life in prison. She bids him wait two years when she will be of age. Strephon is very much against waiting as the Lord Chancellor may marry her himself in the meantime. Also he has noticed that several Peers of the House of Lords have been casting sheep's eyes at her.

None Shall Part Us

Phyllis and Strephon

PHYLLIS None shall part us from each o - ther, One in life and death are
STREPHON All in all since that fond meet - ing When, in joy, I woke to

we, All in all to one an - o - ther, I to
find, Mine the heart with - in thee beat - ing, Mine the

thee and thou to me!___ All in all to one an-
love that heart en - shrined!_ Mine the heart with - in thee

o - ther, I to thee and thou to me!
beat - ing, Mine the love that heart en - shrined!

(PHYLLIS) Thou the tree, and I the flow - er;
Thou the stream, and I the wil - low;

(STREPHON) I the tree thou the flow - er;
I the stream, thou the wil - low

Thou the i - dol, I the throng;
Thou the sculp - tor. I the clay;

I the i - dol, thou the throng;
I the sculp - tor, thou the clay;

Thou the day and I the hour_____ Thou the
Thou the o - cean, I the bil - low_____ Thou the

I the day and thou the hour_____ I the
I the o - cean, thou the bil - low_____ I the

They leave together and a procession of Peers of the House of Lords marches on

March Of The Peers

Chorus of Peers

Allegro maestoso

Bow, bow, ye low-er mid-dle class-es! Bow, bow, ye trades-men, bow, ye mass-es,

Blow the trum-pets, bang the brass-es, Tan-tan - ta - ra, tzing, boom!

Bow, bow, ye low-er mid-dle class-es, Bow, bow, ye trades-men, bow, ye mass-es

Copyright MCMXXXVIII—by Amsco Music Publishing Co.

Blow the trum-pets, bang the brass-es Tan-tan-ta-ra! tzing, boom, tzing, boom!

Tan-tan-ta-ra! tzing, boom, tzing, boom! Tan-tan-ta-ra! tzing, boom, tzing, boom!

Blow, blow the trum-pets, bang the brass-es! Blow, blow the

trum-pets, bang the brass-es! Blow, blow the trum-pets!

cresc.

The Lord Chancellor enters with **pomp** and ceremony followed by his train bearer. He explains his duties as Guardian of pretty maids who are Wards in Chancery.

The Law
Lord Chancellor

After this song the Chancellor tells the Peers that he has called them together to decide which one shall marry Phyllis. He also informs them that he would be glad to marry Phyllis himself but such an action might be misunderstood in regard to his position as Lord Chancellor. Phyllis is brought before them and all the Peers offer themselves in marriage but she refuses them all, confessing that she has already pledged her heart and hand. The Chancellor is furious at this defiance of his authority and demands the name of her lover. At this point Strephon enters and claims her, explaining that the order of Chancery means nothing to him as Nature herself commands him to marry Phyllis. The Chancellor doubts the authority of this and explains his case in pronouncing decisions on all legal matters.

Said I To Myself, Said I

Allegro comodo   Lord Chancellor

I,) I'll___ nev-er as-sume that a rogue or a thief is a
I,) My___ lear-ned pro-fes-sion I'll nev-er dis-grace by
I,) Or as-sume that the wit-ness-es sum-moned in force in Ex-
I,) Pro-fes-sion-al li-cense, if car-ried too far,___ your

gen-tle-man wor-thy im-pli-cit be-lief, Be-cause his at-tor-ney has
tak-ing a fee with a grin on my face, When I have-n't been there to at-
che-quer, Queen's bench, Com-mon Pleas, or Di-vorce Have per-jur'd them-selves as a
chance of pro-mo-tion will cer-tain-ly mar And I fan-cy the rule might ap-

sent me a brief, (Said I to my-self, said I!)
tend to the case, (Said I to my-self, said I!)
mat-ter of course, (Said I to my-self, said I!)
ply to the bar, (Said I to my-self, said I!)

1-2-3   4

The Chancellor forbids Phyllis to marry Strephon and he seeks the help of Iolanthe, his mother. She promises to invoke the aid of the Fairy Queen. Phyllis overhears Strephon's conversation with Iolanthe and becomes jealous, refusing to believe that Iolanthe is Strephon's mother, because Iolanthe, being a fairy, appears to be a young girl. In her anger she offers herself to any one of the Peers. The Fairy Queen and her band of fairies join them seeking to aid Strephon. The Lord Chancellor insults the Fairy Queen and she denounces them all, threatening to send Strephon to Parliament, and through her influence command a majority and thwart every bill and measure they wish to enact. And all bills they wish to kill will be carried in both houses. This would be a drastic annoyance to the noble Peers and they are exceedingly distressed at this threat of the Fairy Queen.

Act II

The second act opens in the courtyard of the Palace of Westminster. Private Willis is on Sentry Duty.

Fal, Lal, La!
Sentry

nev.-er nur-tur'd in the lap of lux-u-ry, yet I ad-mon-ish you I
then the pros-pect of a lot of dull M. P's. in close prox-i-mi-ty, All

am an in-tel-lec-tual chap, and think of things that would as-ton-ish you! I
think-ing for them-selves is what, no man could face with e-qua-nim-i-ty! Then

Tempo I

of-ten think it's com-ic-al, fal, lal,_ la! fal, lal,_ la! How
let's re-joice with loud fal, lal, fal, lal,_ la! fal, lal,_ la! That

na-ture al-ways does con-trive fal, lal, la! la! That_ ev-'ry boy and_

ev - 'ry gal that's born in - to the world a - live, Is ei - ther a lit - tle

lib - er - al, or else a lit - tle con - ser - va - tive! fal, lal, la!

fal, lal, la! Is ei - ther a lit - tle lib - er - al or else a lit - tle con - ser - va

tive! fal, lal, la! When

Celia, Leita and Fleta enter with a group of fairies. They are overjoyed at Strephon's great success as a member of Parliament, where he passes every law he chooses over the heads of all regardless of Whigs or Tories or Lords or Commons. Two Peers from the House of Lords appeal to Celia, Leita and Fleta to use their influence to stop Strephon but they are powerless, although greatly attracted and impressed by the Peers. When they leave, the Fairy Queen, who has overheard the conversation, berates the three fairies for being impressed by mortals. She tells them that even she herself was "very much taken" by Private Willis but that she continually fights the infatuation.

Oh, Foolish Fay

Fairy Queen

love, Re - sem - ble I the am -'rous dove? Re - sem - ble I the am -'rous
draw, In that we gain a Cap-tain Shaw! In that we gain a Cap-tain

dove? Oh, am -'rous dove! Type of o - vi - dius
Shaw! Oh, Cap - tain Shaw! Type of true love kept

na - so! This heart of mine is soft as thine, al -
un - der! Could thy bri - gade with cool cas-cade quench

though I dare not say so! Oh, am -'rous
my great love I won - der! Oh, Cap - tain

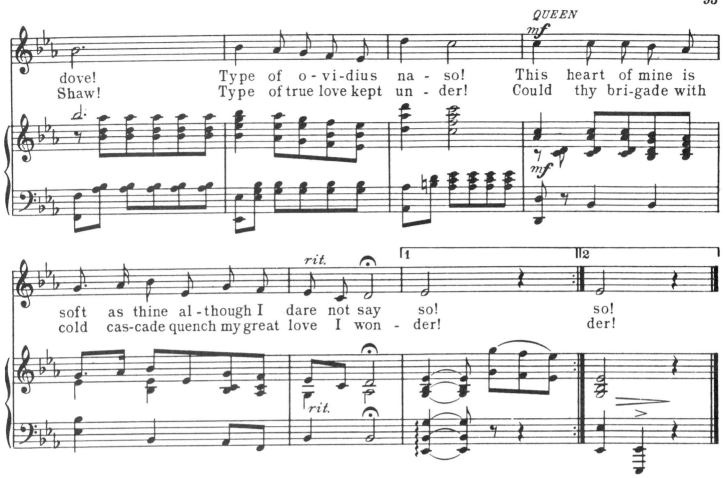

QUEEN

dove! | Type of o-vi-dius na-so! | This heart of mine is
Shaw! | Type of true love kept un-der! | Could thy bri-gade with

soft as thine al-though I dare not say so! | so!
cold cas-cade quench my great love I won-der! | der!

The fairies leave and Phyllis enters. She has betrothed herself to both Lord Mountararat and Lord Tol-loller. These Peers try to persuade her to choose between them but she refuses, as secretly her heart still belongs to Strephon. Strephon finally convinces Phyllis that Iolanthe is really his mother and they ask her to influence the Lord Chancellor to allow them to marry. Iolanthe thereupon pleads with the Lord Chancellor as she promised.

He Loves
Iolanthe

He loves! if in the by-gone years thine eyes have ev-er shed tears

Bit-ter un-a-vail-ing tears for one un-time-ly dead, If in the ev-en

The Chancellor does not accede to Iolanthe's pleading but announces that he himself is going to marry Phyllis. Iolanthe then makes the startling revelation that she herself is the Chancellor's wife and that Strephon is his son. The Fairy Queen thereupon threatens Iolanthe with death for revealing herself to her mortal husband. Celia, Leita and Fleta defiantly announce that they too are engaged to Peers and furthermore all the fairies are engaged to mortals, so if the law is enforced she will have to have everyone put to death. So the Queen relents and agrees to marry Private Willis. Everyone is united with their loved ones and the Opera ends happily.

Finale
Entire Company

wards in Chan - ce - ry _____ He will be sure - ly hap - pier

For he's such a sus - cep - ti - ble chan-cel - lor!

8va

loco

ff

sempre ff

THE PIRATES OF PENZANCE
or
The Slave Of Duty

Libretto by:
W. S. GILBERT

Music by:
SIR ARTHUR SULLIVAN

Cast of Characters

RICHARD . . . . The Pirate King
SAMUEL . . . . The Lieutenant
FREDERIC . . . . The Pirate Apprentice
RUTH . . . . The Piratical Maid of all Work
MAJOR-GENERAL STANLEY
SERGEANT OF POLICE
MABEL ⎫
KATE ⎬ . . . . General Stanley's Daughters
EDITH ⎪
ISABEL⎭

Chorus of Pirates, Maidens, Noblemen, Policemen, etc.
England in the 19th Century.

Act I

The scene is a Rocky Coast near Cornwall. The pirate ship lies at anchor in the background and the pirates themselves have their headquarters in a natural cave in the rocks. They are celebrating the event of Frederic's having finished his apprenticeship and becoming a proficient journeyman pirate. Frederic, however, announces that he is leaving them because being apprenticed to a pirate was a grave mistake. The whole fault lies with Ruth, who was ordered by Frederic's father to apprentice the boy to a "pilot." She being somewhat deaf, misunderstood the word and apprenticed him to a pirate. Frederic tells them that he has no talent for being a pirate and that he has no interest in the business; and furthermore that he intends to devote the rest of his life to their extermination. Ruth begs him to take her with him and he agrees. Never having seen any other woman he does not realize how homely she is. He urges Richard, the pirate King to accompany him back to civilization and make his own extermination unnecessary. The King refuses.

Oh, Better Far To Live And Die
Pirate King and Chorus of Pirates

Oh, better far to live and die Under the brave black flag I fly, Than
sally forth to seek my prey I help myself in a royal way; I

play a sanc - ti - mon-ious part, With a pir - ate head and a pir - ate heart.
sink a few more ships, it's true, Than a well bred mon - arch ought to do!

A-way to the cheat-ing world go you,
But ma-ny a king on a first class throne,

Where pir - ates all _ are well to do, But I'll be true to the song I sing, And
If he wants to call _ his crown his own, Must man-age some-how to get through, More

cresc.

a tempo

live and die a pir - ate king. For _ I am a pir - ate king! _
dir - ty work than ever I do.

f

The Pirates then take advantage of the tide and sail **away** leaving Frederic alone with Ruth. Frederic seems to suspect that Ruth is no beauty and presses her with questions concerning her looks. She insists that she is a "very fine woman." At this point they hear the voices of girls singing in the distance. Frederic climbs up on a high rock and sees a lot of beautiful girls. Ruth realizes that she is lost as Frederic immediately reproaches her for deceiving him about her looks. He hides in a cave as the girls enter.

Climbing Over Rocky Mountain
Chorus of Girls

Climb-ing ov-er rock-y moun-tain, Skip-ping riv-u-let and foun-tain, Pass-ing where the wil-lows qui-ver, Pass-ing where the wil-lows qui-ver, By the ev-er roll-ing riv-er, Swol-len with the sum-mer rain, the sum-mer rain.

The girls prove to be daughters of General Stanley of Her Majesty's Army, who are on a picnic and have wandered away from the General and his servants. They decide to take off their shoes and stockings and go wading but when Frederic sees their intention he immediately reveals himself. When he informs them that he is a pirate they are greatly shocked, but he tells them that this very day he has renounced that criminal profession and asks their indulgence and assistance in returning to his position in the civilized world.

Oh, Is There Not One Maiden

Frederic and Chorus of Girls

He is discouraged and is about to leave them when Mabel, the fairest of the General's daughters, tells him that she feels it is her duty to assist him. Her sisters taunt her saying that if he were not so handsome she would not have "the moral beauty to make worldly interest subordinate to her sense of duty."

Poor Wand'ring One
Mabel and Chorus of Girls

Poor wan - d'ring one,_____ If such poor love_ as mine, Can help thee find true peace of mind, Why, take it, it__ is thine!

cresc.

CHOS. OF GIRLS

Take heart, no dan - ger low'rs, Take an - y heart but ours!

MABEL

p

Take heart, fair days will shine, Take an - y heart, take

mine!

CHOS. OF GIRLS

f

Take heart, no dan - ger low'rs,

Take___ an - y heart but ours! Take heart,

MABEL

p

fair days will shine, take an - y heart, take mine! Ah_____

Frederic and Mabel try to pair off together, but are pestered by the other girls who pretend to talk about the weather but really listen to everthing they say. Suddenly they find themselves surrounded by the pirates, who have unexpectedly returned. Each pirate seizes a maid for himself and announces that this is a golden opportunity to get married. The girls are vastly relieved when General Stanley enters and announces himself as a person of great importance.

I Am the Very Model
General and Chorus

I am the ve - ry mod - el of a
I know our myth - ic his - tor - y, King

mod - ern ma - jor gen - er - al, I've in - for - ma - tion ve - ge - ta - ble,
Ar - thur's and Sir Car - o - doc's, I an - swer hard a - cros - tics, I've a

an - i - mal and min - er - al; I know the kings of Eng - land and I
pret - ty taste for par - a - dox; I quote, in el - e - gi - acs, all the

many cheer-ful facts a-bout the square of the hy - po-ten-use, With ma-ny cheer-ful facts a-bout the
whis-tle all the airs from that in-fer-nal non-sense Pin-a-fore, And whis-tle all the airs from that in-

square of the hy - po-ten-use, With ma-ny cheer-ful facts a-bout the square of the hy - po - ten-po-ten-
fer-nal non-sense Pin-a-fore, And whis-tle all the airs from that in - fer-nal non-sense Pin-a - Pin - a -

MAJOR GENERAL

use.   I'm   ve - ry good at in - te- gral and
fore.   Then   I can write a wash-ing bill in

dif-fer-en-tial cal-cu -lus, I know the sci- en - ti - fic names of be-ings an - i-mal-cu-lous. In
ba-by-lon-ic cu-nei-form, And tell you ev-'ry de-tail of Ca - rac-ta - cus-'s un - i-form.

short, in mat-ters veg-e-ta-ble, an-i-mal, and min-er-al, I am the ve-ry mod-el of a

CHORUS

mod-ern ma-jor gin-er-al. In short, in mat-ters veg-e-ta-ble, an-i-mal, and min-er-al, He

is the ve-ry mod-el of a mod-ern ma-jor gin-er-al! mod-ern ma-jor gin-er-al.

The Pirates of Penzance, all being orphans, have an ironclad rule that when any prisoner is discovered to be an orphan, they are immediately released. When the General is informed that he and his daughters are prisoners of the Pirates of Penzance and that the pirates, being bachelors, intend to marry his daughters, he tells them that he is an orphan. The pirates are disappointed but according to their custom they release the General and his daughters and allow them to depart. Frederic goes with them and leaves Ruth, his former nurse, behind with the pirates.

Act II

The second act takes place in the ancestral hall of the General's ancient castle. The General is discovered with his daughters bemoaning the fact that he deceived the pirates by claiming to be an orphan. Frederic enters and points out that the pirates would have undoubtedly married his whole family, had he not done so. This seems to soothe the General's conscience and Frederic informs them that he is about to lead his band of policemen on an expedition against the pirates. At this moment the policemen enter resplendent in bright new uniforms with brass buttons, enthusiastic to start the crusade against the pirates.

Policemen's Chorus
Sergeant and Chorus of Policemen

When the foe-man bares his steel, Ta-ran-ta-ra, ta-ran-ta-ra! We un-com-for-ta-ble feel! Ta-ran-ta-ra, And we find the wis-est thing, Ta-ran-ta-ra, ta-ran-ta-ra! Is to slap our chests and sing ta-ran-ta-ra! For when threat-'nd with e-meutes ta-ran-ta-ra, ta-ran-ta-ra, And your heart is in your boots ta-ran-ta-

They all march off, leaving Frederic alone. He is congratulating himself on the fine job he is about to do in exterminating the pirates, when he suddenly finds himself cornered by Ruth and the Pirate King with a pistol at each of his ears. They show him his apprenticeship papers and command him to listen to a startling revelation.

For Some Ridiculous Reason
Pirate King

For some ridiculous reason, to which, However, I've no desire to be dis- loyal, Some person in authority — I don't know who — very likely the astronomer royal, has decided that, although for such a beastly month as February, Twenty-eight days as a general rule are plenty: One year in four his days shall be reckoned as nine and twenty. Through some singular coincidence, I shouldn't be surprised if it were owing to the agency of an ill-natured fairy, You are the victim of this clumsy arrangement, having been born in leap year on the twenty-ninth of February. And so, by a simple arithmetical process, you'll easily discover that, though you've lived twenty one years, Yet if we go by birthdays, you're only five and a little bit ov-er!

Frederic feels that he is duty-bound to go back to the pirates and being so bound tells them that General Stanley deceived them when he said that he was an orphan. The Pirate King swears vengeance against the General for the trick he played and determines to storm the castle that night. Ruth and the Pirate King leave, and Mabel enters. Frederic tells her that he is still legally apprenticed to the pirates on account of his birthday being the 29th of February and bids her good-bye.

Oh, Leave Me Not to Pine
Mabel and Fred

Mabel is left alone and the Sergeant of Police enters in search of Frederic. Mabel tells him Frederic has discovered that he is still legally bound to the Pirates and has rejoined them through a sense of duty. Strangely enough the Sergeant is sympathetic and reveals that he really has a tender feeling for criminals.

When a Felon's Not Engaged

Sergeant and Chorus of Policemen

The Sergeant suspects that the pirates are about to attack, so he bids everyone hide. They have no sooner concealed themselves when the pirates march in, armed to the teeth, with Richard, their King, leading them.

Pirate Chorus
Chorus of Pirates, Chorus of Policemen

PIRATES

ra!   So steal-thi - ly the pi - rate creeps, While all the house-hold sound-ly sleeps.

Come,   friends, who plough the sea,

Truce to na-vi-ga-tion, take an-oth-er sta - tion, Let's va - ry pi - ra - cee,

with a lit-tle bur-gla - ree!   Come,   friends who plough the sea,

Truce to na-vi-ga-tion, take an-oth-er sta-tion, Let's va-ry pi-ra-cee

with a lit-tle bur-gla-ree, With cat-like tread up-on our prey we

steal; In si-lence dread our cau-tious way

we feel.

The General enters from one side and his daughters from the other, all in night attire and carrying candles. The pirates seize the General and overcome the police, but when the Sergeant commands them to surrender "In the Name of Queen Victoria", they immediately yield and submit to arrest. Ruth, the piratical maid of all work now makes the revelation that these are not actually pirates at all but really noblemen who have gone wrong, all members of the House of Peers in disguise. Thereupon the General pardons them all, Frederic and Mabel are once more united and all ends happily.

THE GONDOLIERS
or
The King Of Barataria

Libretto by
W. S. GILBERT

Music by
SIR ARTHUR SULLIVAN

Cast of Characters

MARCO PALMIERI }
GIUSEPPI PALMIERI } The Gondoliers
DON ALHAMBRA DEL BOLERO, Grand Inquisitor of Venice
DUKE OF PLAZA-TORO, Spanish Grandee
DUCHESS OF PLAZA-TORO
CASILDA, their daughter
LUIZ, their attendant
INEZ, Luiz' mother, also the King's foster-mother
GIANETTA }
TESSA } flower girls

The Scene is Venice and Barataria.   Time about 1750

Act I

The opera opens in the Piazzetta at Venice. The Duke's palace is on the right. A group of flower girls are making bouquets of roses for Marco and Giuseppe, who have announced their intention of selecting their brides from among them this very day. The girls greet them with a great display of enthusiasm.

We're Called Gondolieri
Marco and Giuseppe

Allegro con brio

1. We're called ____ Gon-do-lier-i, but that's a va-ga-ry It's quite hon-or-a-ry, the
gal - lant-ry not-ed since we were short coat-ed, To la-dies de-vo-ted my

trade that we ply_____
broth-er and I!_____

2. For

When morn-ing is break-ing, our couch-es for - sak-ing, To greet their a - wak-ing with

car-ols we come. At sum-mer day's moon-ing, when wea-ry la-goon-ing, Our man - do-lins

tun - ing, we la - - zi - ly ___ thrum Our __

man - do - lins ___ tun-ing, we la - zi-ly thrum Tra la la la la la

la, Tra la la la la la la, Tra la la la la, Tra la la la la, Tra la la la la la! When ves-

pers are ring-ing, to hope ev-er cling-ing, With songs of our sing-ing a vi-gil we

keep. _____

We're called Gon-

Marco and Giuseppe declare that they are ready to select their brides, but do not wish to do so before all of them, as they want to be absolutely impartial. So a game of "Blind Man's Buff" is suggested and the gay gondoliers submit to being blindfolded, agreeing to marry the two girls they catch. The merry game begins and the gondoliers catch Gianetta and Tessa, and they are duly betrothed. They depart and the Duke of Plaza-Toro, his wife and daughter enter with their attendant Luiz. Their costumes are rich and pompous but old and faded. The Duke is telling his daughter that she was married by proxy to the heir to the throne of Barataria over twenty years ago. The old King being dead, they must find the Prince, who was stolen when a boy by the Grand Inquisitor of Venice because the King had become a Methodist. The Duke reveals that he intends to visit the Grand Inquisitor so they can locate the boy and place him on the throne where he rightfully belongs. This will automatically make his daughter Casilda, the Queen of Barataria.

In Enterprise Of Martial Kind
The Duke

The Duke and Duchess exit into the palace. The Duke's revelations leave Casilda and Luiz. in a state of utter bewilderment as, unbeknown to the Duke and Duchess, they are deeply in love with each other.

There Was A Time
Casilda and Luiz

The Duke and Duchess re-enter with the Grand Inquisitor himself, Don Alhámbra del Bolero. He tells them that the Crown-Prince is in Venice, where he has adopted the vocation of a gondolier.

I Stole A Prince

Don Alhambra

Allegretto non troppo vivo

1. I stole the Prince and I brought him here, And left him, gai - ly prat - tling, With a high - ly re - spect - a - ble gon - do - lier, Who prom-ised the roy - al babe to rear, And teach him the trade of a

sped and when at the end of a year, I ___ sought that in - fant cher - ish'd, That high - ly re - spect - a - ble gon - do - lier, Was ly - ing a corpse on his hum - ble bier, I dropp'd a Grand In

ow - ing I'm dis - posed to fear, To his ter - ri - ble taste for tip - pling, That high - ly re - spect - a - ble gon - do - lier, Could nev - er de - clare with a mind sin - cere, Which of the two was his

chil - dren fol - lowed his old ca - reer, This state-ment can't be par - ried, Of a high - ly re - spect - a - ble gon - do - lier, Well one of the two (who will soon be here) But which of the two ___ is

ti - mo - neer, With his own be - lov - ed brat - ling. But both the babes were
qui - si - tor's tear, That gon - do - lier had per - ish'd. A taste for drink, com -
off - spring dear, And which the roy - al strip - ling. Which was which he
not quite clear, Is the roy - al Prince you mar - ried. Search in and out and

strong_ and stout And con - sid - er - ing all things clev - er. Of that there is no
bined_ with gout, Had dou - bled him up for - ev - er. Of that there is no
ne'er could make out, De - spite his best en - deav - or Of that there is no
'round a - bout, And you'll dis - cov - er nev - er. A tale so free from

man - ner of doubt No prob - a - ble, pos - si - ble sha - dow of doubt, No pos - si - ble doubt what -
man - ner of doubt No prob - a - ble, pos - si - ble sha - dow of doubt, No pos - si - ble doubt what -
man - ner of doubt No prob - a - ble, pos - si - ble sha - dow of doubt, No pos - si - ble doubt what -
ev - er - y doubt All prob - a - ble, pos - si - ble sha - dow of doubt, All pos - si - ble doubt what -

1-2-3   mf 4

ev - er.
ev - er.
ev - er. No pos - si - ble doubt what - ev - er!
ev - er.

2. Time
3. But
4. The

ev - er!

f   mf

Casilda sees a ray of hope in the fact that they are not really sure of the identity of the Prince, but Don Alhambra tells her that he has sent for Luiz' mother, who was also foster-mother of the Prince, to learn the truth. At this time Marco and Giuseppe enter with Gianetta and Tessa and flower girls. They have been married and are celebrating the event with dancing and singing.

When A Merry Maiden Marries
Tessa

When a mer-ry maid-en mar-ries, Sor-row goes and plea-sure tar-ries; Ev-'ry sound be-comes a song, All is right and noth-ing's wrong! From to-day and ev-er af-ter Let our tears be tears of laugh-ter, Ev-'ry sigh that finds a vent Be a sigh of sweet con-tent! When you mar-ry mer-ry maid-en,

Don Alhambra recognizes Marco and Giuseppe as the sons of Baptisto Palmieri, with whom he had left the Crown Prince twenty years before. He informs them that one of them is the King of Barataria, but as he is not sure which one it is, they are to rule jointly until positive identification of the real Prince can be established. Tessa and Gianetta are delighted because one of them will be Queen of Barataria.

Then One Of Us Will Be A Queen
Quartette

1. Then one of us will be ___ a Queen, and ___ sit on a gold-en throne; With a crown in-stead of a hat on her head, And di - a-monds all her own! With a beau-ti-ful robe of gold and green, I've al - ways un-der-stood; I won-der wheth-er she'd wear a feath-er? I rath - er think she

drive a-bout in a car-riage and pair, with the King on her left-hand side; And a milk-white horse as a mat-ter of course, When-ev - er she wants to ride! With beau-ti-ful sil-ver shoes to wear, Up - on her dain-ty feet; With end-less stocks of beau-ti-ful frocks, And as much as she wants to

should!
eat!   Oh!___ 'tis a glo-rious thing, I ween, to be a reg-u-lar Roy-al Queen! No

half and half af - fair,   I mean, No half and half af - fair, But a right down, reg-u-lar

reg-u-lar, reg-u-lar, reg-u-lar Roy- al Queen!   2 She'll Queen! Oh, 'tis a glo-rious

thing, I ween, to be a reg-u-lar Roy-al Queen, a right-down reg-u-lar Roy - al   Queen.

Tessa and Gianetta are to be disappointed however, for Don Alhambra informs them that they will have to re-main in Venice for the present. A boat docks at the quay and bidding their brides a sad farewell the joint kings embark for Barataria, followed by other gondoliers and Don Alhambra.

Act II

The second act is at the Court of Barataria. Marco and Giuseppe, in royal raiment are seated on twin thrones. They are engaged in cleaning the Royal Crown and Sceptre, as these duties would be beneath the dignity of the nobility. The gondoliers who came from Venice with them have become courtiers. Marco and Giuseppe are yearning for the brides they left in Venice, when suddenly Tessa and Gianetta themselves and all the flower girls arrive. The twin gondolier Kings are delighted and immediately order a grand ball and banquet in honor of this happy re-union.

Dance A Cachucha
Chorus

Dance a ca-chu-cha, fan-dan-go, bo-le-ro, Xe-res we'll drink, Man-za-nil-la, Mon-te-ro; Wine when it runs in a-bun-dance, en-han-ces the

pat - ter, we'll dance! Old Xe - res we'll drink Man-za - nil - la, Mon - te - ro, For wine when it

runs in a - bun-dance En - han - ces the reck - less de - light of that

wild-est of dan-ces, The reck-less de-light of that wild-est of dan - -

ces _____

In the midst of the festivities, Don Alhambra suddenly appears and voices his disapproval of the presence of the brides and the flower girls. Everyone is abashed and even Marco and Giuseppe are embarrassed. The other revelers run off. Don Alhambra demands an explanation as to why the footmen and grooms were dancing with the ladies of the court. Marco and Giuseppe announce that it is in accordance with their new democratic principles. Don Alhambra disapproves of such goings-on and predicts only failure for such an experiment.

There Lived A King
Don Alhambra

in his face, And in his heart he found a — place, For all the er - ring
up like hay, Prime Min - is - ters and such as — they, Grew like as - par - a -
ly fore-told, When ev - 'ry bless - ed thing you hold, Is made of sil - ver,

hu - man race, And ev - 'ry wretch-ed fel-low. When he had Rhen-ish wine to drink, It
gus in May, And Dukes were three a pen-ny. On ev - 'ry side Field Mar-shal's gleam'd, Small
or of gold, You long for sim - ple pew-ter. When you have noth-ing else to wear, But

made him ver - y sad to think that some at jun-ket or at jink, Must be con-tent with
beer were Lords Lieu-ten-ant deem'd, with Ad - mi-rals the o - cean teem'd, All 'round his wild do -
cloth of gold and sa-tins rare, for cloth of gold you cease to care, Up goes the price of

tod - dy, With tod - dy, tod - dy. He
min - ious, 'With Ad - mi - rals a - round his do - min - ious. And
shod - dy, Of shod - dy, shod - dy. In

The Grand Inquisitor now tells Marco and Giuseppe that one of them—he doesn't know which, but the one who is the Crown Prince—was married by proxy twenty years before to Casilda the daughter of the Duke de Plaza Toro. The Duke and Duchess, now lavishly costumed, enter with Casilda. The Duke introduces his daughter to Marco and Giuseppe and tells her she will soon know which one is her husband. He complains that he is shocked at the absence of pomp and ceremony and lack of formality at this court.

I Am A Courtier

Quintet

Tempo di Gavotte

DUKE

1. I am a court-ier grave and se-rious, Who is a-bout to kiss your hand, Try to com-
votte per-form se-date-ly, Of-fer your hand with con-scious pride, Take an

MARCO and GIUSEPPE

bine a pose im-pe-rious, With a de-mean-our no-bly bland, Let us com-
at-ti-tude not too state-ly, Still suf-fi-cient-ly dig-ni-fied. Now for an

DUKE

bine a pose im-pe-rious, With a de-mean-our no-bly bland. That's if
at-ti-tude not too state-ly, Still suf-fi-cient-ly dig-ni-fied. Once-ly

an - y-thing, too un-bend-ing, Too ag-gress-ive-ly___ stiff and grand; Now to the
twice - ly, once-ly, twice-ly, Bow im-press-ive-ly___ 'ere you glide; Ca-pi-tal,

CASILDA and

oth-er ex-treme you're tend-ing, Don't be so deuc-ed-ly con-de-scend-ing! Now to the
both, you've caught it nice-ly That is the sort of___ thing pre-cise-ly! Cap-i-tal,

DUCHESS

oth-er ex-treme you're tend-ing, Don't be so dread-ful-ly con-de-scend-ing!
both, they've caught it ___ nice-ly, That is the sort of___ thing pre-cise-ly!

MARCO and GIUSEPPE

Oh, sweet to earn a no-ble-man's praise! Ca-pi-tal both, Ca-pi-tal both we've caught it

144

nice - ly. Sup-pos-ing he's right in what he says, This is the style of thing pre-

cise - ly.   2. Now_ a ga- cise - ly. Cap - i -tal both,

Cap - i -tal both, you've caught it nice -ly! That is the style of thing pre-cise-ly! That is the

style of thing, the style_____ of thing pre - cise - ly!

Finally, Luiz' mother, who was the foster mother of the real Crown Prince, is brought in and she proceeds to straighten out the whole matter for good and all. She announces that neither Marco nor Giuseppe is of royal lineage and that the real Crown Prince, who is now the King of Barataria, is none other than Luiz. Casilda and Luiz are delighted, as are Marco, Giuseppe, Tessa and Gianetta, and everything ends with happiness for all.

Finale
Entire Company

So good-bye, ca - chu-cha, fan-dan-go, bo-

le-ro, We'll dance a fare-well to that meas-ure___ Old Xe-res, a-dieu, Man-za-nil-la, Mon-

te-ro, We leave you with feel-ings of pleas-ure! Once more___ gon-do-lier - i, both

skil-ful and wa-ry, Free from this quan-da-ry, con-ten-ted are we,___ Ah!___

Ah! _____ Once more __ gon-do-lier-i, gon-do-

lier - i, __ gon-do - lier - i, con-ten-ted are we! So

good-bye, ca-chu-cha, fan-d an-go, bo - le-ro, We'll dance a fare-well to that meas-ure. Old

Xe - res, a-dieu, Man-za-nil -la, Mon-te - ro, We leave you with feel-ings of pleas-ure, with

feel-ings of pleas ure! __

PATIENCE
or
Bunthorne's Bride

Libretto by
W. S. GILBERT

Music by
SIR ARTHUR SULLIVAN

Cast of Characters

REGINALD BUNTHORNE, a fleshly poet
ARCHIBALD GROSVENOR, an idyllic poet
COLONEL CALVERLEY
MAJOR MURGATROYD } Officers of the Dragoons
LIEUT., DUKE OF DUNSTABLE
LADY ANGELA
LADY SAPHIR { Love-sick
LADY ELLA { Maidens
LADY JANE
PATIENCE, the village milk-maid

The Scene — England, about 1870

Act I

The first scene of the opera is the entrance to Bunthorne's castle. A bevy of young ladies is singing a love-sick ditty. They are arrayed in Grecian costumes and are accompanying themselves on guitars and mandolins. They are in despair over the fact that Bunthorne remains totally oblivious to their amorous feelings for him. Moreover, Lady Jane tells them that Bunthorne's fancy has turned to Patience, a dairy-maid. Patience herself enters at this time and gazes with pity at the lovesick girls. Never having been in love herself she doubts the desirability of it, if it brings such misery.

I Cannot Tell
Patience

1. I can-not tell what this love may be, That com-eth to
2. If love is a thorn they show no wit, Who fool-ish-ly

all but not to me; It can-not be kind, as they'd im-ply, Or why do these
hug and fos-ter it; If love is a weed, how sim-ple they, Who gath-er it

la - dies sigh? It can-not be joy_ and rap-ture deep, Or why do these
day by day! If love is a net-tle that makes you smart, Then why do you

gen-tle la-dies weep? It can-not be bliss-ful as 'tis said, Or why are their
wear it next your heart? And if it be none of these say I,_ Ah, why do you

eyes so won-d'rous red?
sit and sob and sigh?

Tho' ev - 'ry

rit. e dim.   *a tempo*   *mf*

la la la la la la la la la la la la and mi - se - rie!

The girls tell Patience that if she has never loved she does not know the true meaning of happiness. Naturally she doubts this, having witnessed their despondency. She announces that a company of Dragoons have stopped in the village and are waiting for the girls, but they are not interested and enter the Castle. The dragoons' officers enter at this time and sing of the remarkable prowess of a heavy dragoon.

If You Want A Receipt
Chorus of Dragoons and Colonel Calverly

If you want a re-ceipt for that pop-u-lar mys-te-ry Known to the world as a

CHOS.

hea-vy dra-goon Yes Yes Yes Yes Yes Yes Yes Take

all the re-mark-a-ble peo-ple in his-to-ry, Rat-tle them off to a pop-u-lar tune!

CHOS.

Yes Yes Yes Yes Yes Yes Yes.

1. The pluck of Lord Nel-son on board of the vic-to-ry Gen-ius of Bis-marck de-
want a re-ceipt for this sol-dier-like par-a-gon, Get at the wealth of the

segue

vis- ing a plan; The hum-or of Field-ing(which sounds con-tra-dic -to -ry) Cool-ness of Pa - get a -
Czar (if you can) The fam-i -ly pride of a Span - iard from A - ra-gon, Force of Me-phis-to pro-

bout to tre-pan, The sci-ence of Ju-lien the em - i -nent mu-si -co Wit of Mac- au-ley who
nounc-ing a ban, A smack of Lord Wat-er-ford, reck-less and rol-lick-y, Swag-ger of Rod-er-ick,

wrote of Queen Anne,The pa-thos of Pad-dy, as ren-der'd by Bou-ci-cault, Style of a Bish-op of
head-ing his clan, The keen pen-e-tra-tion of Pad-ding-ton Pol-la -ky, Grace of an o - da-lisque

So-dor and man,The dash of a D'Or-say, di - vest-ed of quack-er - y, Nar - ra-tive pow-ers of
on a di-van, The gen-ius stra-te-gic of Cae-sar or Han - ni-bal, Skill of Sir Gar-net in

Dick - ens and Thack - er - ay, Vic - tor Em - man - u - el, peak haunt - ing Pe - ve - ril,
thrash - ing a can - ni - bal, Fla - vor of Ham - let, the stran - ger, a touch of him,

Tho - mas A - qui - nas and Doc - tor Sa - che - ve - rell Tup - per and Ten - ny - son, Dan - iel De - foe,
Lit - tle of Man - fred (but not ve - ry much of him) Bea - dle of Bur - ling - ton, Ri - chard - son's show,

An - tho - ny Trol - lope and Mis - ter Gui - zot. _____ Ah! _____
Mis - ter Mi - caw - ber and Ma - dame Tus - saud. _____

cresc.

Take of these el - e - ments all that is fu - si - ble melt 'em all down in a

f

pip-kin or cru-ci-ble. Set 'em to sim-mer and take off the scum,__ And a hea-vy dra-

goon is the re - si - du-um! 2. If you um!

Bunthorne enters, followed by the adoring young ladies. He is pretending to be absorbed in writing a poem. The young ladies ignore the dragoons, much to their astonishment and indignation. The dragoons angrily remind the girls that they are engaged, but the girls tell them that they and their uniforms are altogether to commonplace and the dragoons depart, furiously angry. Bunthorne, left alone, admits that he is a fraud, that his aesthetic pose is all a sham and only assumed to attract the adulation of the ladies, because it tickles his vanity. When Patience comes back, Bunthorne drops this aesthetic pretense and tries to persuade her to care for him, but she is not impressed at all and declines his advances. He departs and Lady Angela enters. She finally convinces Patience that love is the most important thing in the world, and Patience decides to fall in love with the first man she meets. Archibald Grosvenor, the idyllic poet enters at this time and immediately inquires if Patience has a lover.

Prithee, Pretty Maiden
Grosvenor and Patience

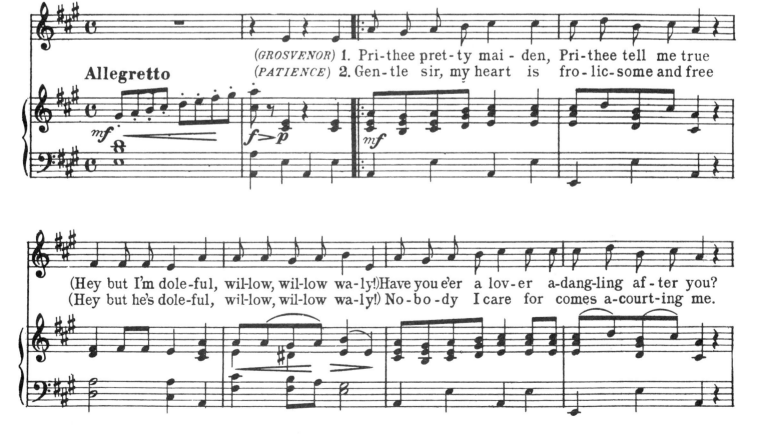

Allegretto

(GROSVENOR) 1. Pri-thee pret-ty mai - den, Pri-thee tell me true
(PATIENCE) 2. Gen-tle sir, my heart is fro-lic-some and free

(Hey but I'm dole-ful, wil-low, wil-low wa-ly!) Have you e'er a lov-er a-dang-ling af-ter you?
(Hey but he's dole-ful, wil-low, wil-low wa-ly!) No-bo-dy I care for comes a-court-ing me.

Patience admires his good looks and admits that she loves him. However, she does not feel any pain or despondency such as she saw the lovesick maidens suffering for Bunthorne. Bunthorne enters and announces that he intends to raffle himself off and give the proceeds to any deserving charity. The ladies all rush to buy tickets but Patience tears them up and announces that she herself will be Bunthorne's bride, not because she loves him but because she wants to be unselfish and sacrifice herself. The ladies turn to the dragoons to be comforted. This only lasts until Grosvenor re-enters, when they are all fascinated by him. Greatly to the disgust of the dragoons they all confess their love for Grosvenor.

Act II

The scene is a forest glade near a beautiful lake. Lady Jane is unhappy because everyone has deserted Bunthorne for Grosvenor, his poetical rival. However, she knows that she herself will remain true. She plays the Cello as an accompaniment to her song.

Silver'd Is The Raven Hair
Lady Jane

Hol - low is the laugh-ter free, Spec-ta-cled the lim-pid eye,
Stout - er than I used to be, Still more cor-pu-lent grow I,

cresc.

dim.

Lit - tle will be left of __ me, In the com-ing bye and bye!
There will be too much of __ me, In the com-ing bye and bye!

Lit - tle will be left of me, In the com-ing_bye and bye!
There will be too much of me, In the com-ing_bye and

mf

1.

2.

bye!

Grosvenor enters, followed by the adoring young ladies singing and playing on their lutes and mandolins. Grosvenor, however, is really in love with Patience, who has foolishly pledged herself to Bunthorne. The lovesick maidens try to force their love upon him, but he tells them as delicately as he can why he can never love any of them.

A Magnet Hung In A Hardware Shop

Grosvenor

Allegretto

ff

1. A mag-net hung in a hard-ware shop, and all a-round was a lov-ing crop, Of
   ir-on and steel ex-press'd sur-prise, the nee-dles o-pen'd their well drill'd eyes, The

scis-sors and nee-dles, nails and knives, of-f'ring love for all their lives
pen-knives felt "shut up," no doubt the scis-sor's de-clar'd them-selves "cut out,"

But for ir-on the mag-net felt no whim,
The ket-tles, they boiled with rage,'tis said,

Tho' he charm-ed ir-on, it charm'd not him, From
While ev-'ry nail went off its head, And

nee-dles and nails and knives he'd turn, for he'd set his love___ on a sil-ver
hi-ther and thi-ther be-gan to roam, Till a ham-mer came up___ and_drove them

churn! A sil-ver churn! A sil-ver churn!
home! It drove them home! It drove them home!

His most aes-the-tic, ve-ry mag-ne-tic fan-cy took this turn, If
While this mag-ne-tic, pe-ri-pa-te-tic lov-er liv'd to learn, By

I can whee-dle a knife or a nee-dle why not a sil-ver churn? His
no en-dea-vor can mag - net ev - er at-tract a' sil-ver churn While

most aes-the-tic, ve-ry mag-ne-tic, fan-cy took this turn, If
this mag-ne-tic, pe-ri-pa-te-tic, lov-er liv'd to learn, By

I can whee-dle a knife or a nee-dle, why not a sil-ver churn. And
no en-dea-vor can mag - net ev-er at-tract a sil-ver churn.

The girls depart. Patience enters and asks Grosvenor if he still loves her. When he tells her that he loves her dearly, she admits that though she feels it her duty to love Bunthorne, she is very miserable in his company Grosvenor tries to embrace her but she repulses him and he sorrowfully leaves her. Bunthorne enters and finds her weeping. He accuses her of being in love with Grosvenor and claims she does not even know what true. love is.

Love Is A Plaintive Song
Patience

1. Love is a plain-tive song,
2. Ren-der-ing good for ill,

Allegretto

Sung by a suf-f'ring maid, Tell-ing a tale of wrong,
Smil-ing at ev-'ry frown, Yield-ing your own self will,

Tell-ing of hope be-tray'd. Tun'd to each chang-ing note,
Laugh-ing your tear-drops down. Nev-er a self-ish whim,

Sor-ry when he is sad, Blind to his ev-'ry mote, Mer -
Trou-ble or pain to stir, Ev-er-y-thing for him, Noth -

ry when he_ is glad! Mer - ry when he_ is glad!
ing at all_ for her! Noth - ing at all_ for her!

Love that no wrong can cure, Love that is al-ways new, That is the love that's
Love that will aye en-dure, Tho' the re-wards be few, That is the love that's

pure, That is the love __ that's true! Love that no wrong can cure,
pure, That is the love __ that's true! Love that will aye en-dure,

Love that is al - ways new, That is the love that's pure, That ____ is the
Tho' the re-wards be few,

love, the love that's true.

Patience leaves in tears. Lady Jane has been following Bunthorne incessantly and he tells her that Grosvenor has stolen all his popularity and that he is going to order him to clear out as he, Bunthorne, intends to again enjoy his former popularity. The dragoons have discarded their uniforms for aesthetic dress, with the hearty approval of the ladies. Bunthorne and Grosvenor meet and Bunthorne, after much discussion, persuades Grosvenor to change his general appearance by cutting his hair, changing his costume, etc., so that he will be entirely commonplace.

When I Go Out Of Door
Bunthorne and Grosvenor

Grosvenor dances off the stage and Bunthorne decides to reform himself and never again commit an ill-natured act. Patience comes in and he tells her of his resolution to become a perfect being. To his surprise Patience then tells him that she will not marry him because there would be no unselfishness in marrying a perfect man. At this moment Grosvenor enters with his hair cut short and dressed in ordinary clothes. The ladies are dancing around him but as he has discarded his aestheticism they all go back to their waiting dragoons. Patience goes to Grosvenor and Lady Jane to the Duke of Dunstable. This leaves Bunthorne with no one at all so he decides to live and die a bachelor. And thus the opera ends.

Finale
Entire Company

much de-bate in-ter-nal, I on La-dy Jane de-cide, Sa-phir now may take the Col-'nel An-gy be the Ma-jor's bride. In that case un-pre-ce-dent-ed, sin-gle I must live and die, I shall have to be con-tent-ed with a tu-lip or li-ly! He will have to be con-tent-ed with a

ALL

tu - lip or li - ly!   In that

case un-pre-ce-dent-ed, sin-gle he must live and die: He will have to be con-tent-ed with a

tu - lip or li - ly! Great - ly pleas'd with one an-oth-er, to get mar-ried we_de-cide: Each of

us will wed the oth-er no-bo-dy be Bun-thornes bride!

rit.   a tempo

TRIAL BY JURY

Libretto by
W. S. GILBERT

Music by
SIR ARTHUR SULLIVAN

Cast of Characters

THE JUDGE
ANGELINA . . The Plaintiff
EDWIN . . . . The Defendant
PLAINTIFF'S COUNSEL
USHER
FOREMAN OF THE JURY
ASSOCIATE JUDGE
A BRIDESMAID

The Scene—A London Courtroom.   Time— About 1875

Act I

The entire action of this one act Operetta takes place in a London Courtroom. The scene, as the opera opens, is typical of the English Court, making ready for the business of the day. The case about to be tried is a breach of promise suit, in which Angelina is suing Edwin

Opening Chorus
Edwin, sued by Angelina

Chorus

Hark! the hour of ten is sound-ing, Hearts with anx-ious fears re-bound-ing, Hall of Jus-tice crowds sur-round-ing, Breath-ing hope and fear. For to-day in this a-re-na

Sum-moned by a stern sub-poe-na, Ed-win, sued by An-ge-li-na, short-ly will ap-

pear. For to-day in this a-re-na, Sum-moned by a stern sub-

poe-na, Ed-win, sued by An-ge-li-na, Short-ly will ap-pear, Ed-win,

sued by An-ge-li-na, short-ly will ap-pear. Hark! the hour of

ten is sound-ing, Hearts with anx-ious fears are sound - ing, Hall of Jus-tice

crowds sur-round-ing, breath-ing hope and fear. For to-day in this a-re-na,

sum-moned by a stern sub-poe-na, Ed-win, sued by An-ge-li-na, short-ly will ap-

pear. Hark! the hour of ten is sound-ing, Hearts with anx-ious fears are

bound-ing, Hall of Jus-tice crowds sur-round-ing, Breath-ing hope ____

and ____ fear. ____

The usher swears in the jury instructing them to set aside all prejudice for either side, and then reveals that he himself is bitterly prejudiced against Edwin, the defendant. Edwin enters carrying a guitar and announces that he is the defendant. The jury shake their fists at him and let him know that they intend to make him feel the weight of the law. Edwin, however, assures them that they will feel entirely different about him when they have heard his side of the story.

When First My Old, Old Love I Knew

Edwin

1. When first my old, old love I knew, my bos - om swelled with
joy in - ces - sant palls the sense, and love un - changed will

joy;   My rich - es at her feet_ I threw, I was a love_ sick
cloy;   And she be - came a bore_ in - tense, un -to a love_ sick

boy!   No terms seem'd too_ ex - trav - a - gant, Up - on her to_ em-
boy!   With fit - ful glim - mer burnt my flame, And I grew cold_ and

rit. e cresc.

ploy, __ I used to mope and sigh and pant, __ just like a love - sick
coy, __ At last one morn - ing I be - came an - oth - er's love - sick

mf a tempo

boy! _____ Tink a tank, tink a tank, tink a tank,   Tink a
boy! _____

tank, tink a tank, tink a tank, I used to mope and
At last one morn-ing

sigh and pant__ just like a love-sick boy! 2. But
I__ be-came an-oth-er's love-sick boy!

The jury admit they were all the same when they were young men, but since they are middle-aged now, they have no patience in such matters. The Usher announces the arrival of the Judge and all address him with great respect and ceremony. This flatters his vanity and he tells them how he was first called to the bar and became a learned Judge.

When I, Good Friends, Was Called To The Bar

The Judge

Moderato

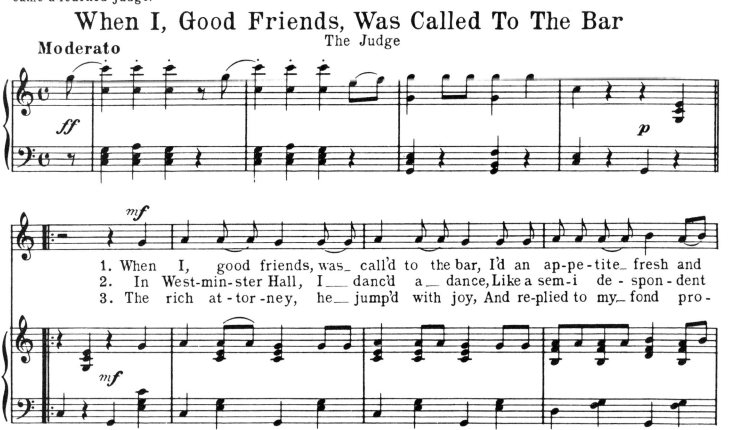

1. When I, good friends, was_ call'd to the bar, I'd an ap-pe-tite_ fresh and
2. In West-min-ster Hall, I__ danc'd a_ dance, Like a sem-i de - spon-dent
3. The rich at-tor-ney, he__ jump'd with joy, And re-plied to my_ fond pro-

heart-y, But_ I was as man-y young bar - ris-ters are, An im-pe - cu - ni-ous
fur - y, For I tho't I should nev - er_ hit on a chance, Of ad-dress-ing_ a_ Brit-ish
fes-sions, "You shall reap the re - ward of your pluck, my_ boy, At the Bai-ley and Mid - dle-sex

part - y.   I'd a swal-low-tail coat_ of a beau-ti-ful blue, A__
jur - y.   But I soon got tir - ed of_ third - class jour - neys And
ses - sions.   You'll soon get used_ to her looks," said he, "And a

brief which I bought of a boob - y; A__ coup - le of shirts and a
din - ners of bread and wa - ter; So I fell in love with a
ver - y nice girl you'll find her; She may ver - y well pass for_

CHORUS

col - lar or_ two, and a ring that_ looked like a ru - by. He'd a
rich at - tor - neys el - der - ly, ug - ly_ daugh - ter. So he
for - ty_ three, in the dusk with a light be - hind her." She has

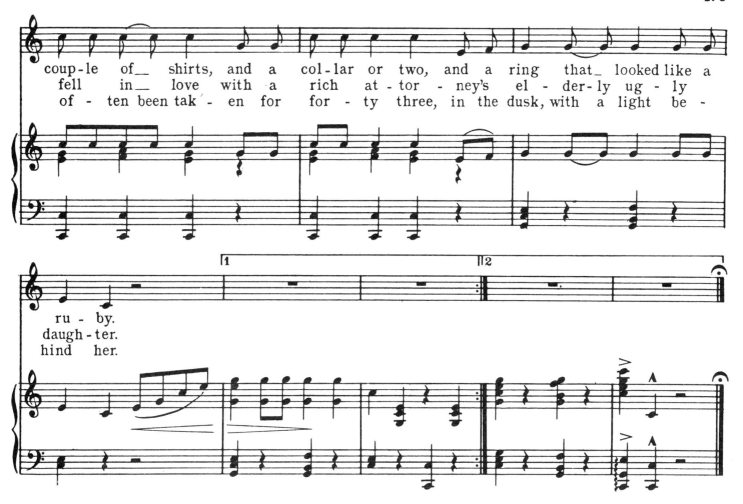

coup-le of__ shirts, and a col-lar or two, and a ring that__ looked like a
fell in__ love with a rich at-tor-ney's el-der-ly ug-ly
of-ten been tak'-en for for-ty three, in the dusk, with a light be -

ru - by.
daugh - ter.
hind her.

The Counsel for the plaintiff enters and the Usher summons Angelina, who enters with her bridesmaids all carrying wreaths of flowers. They are endeavoring to console Angelina.

Comes The Broken Flower
Bridesmaids

Allegro grazioso

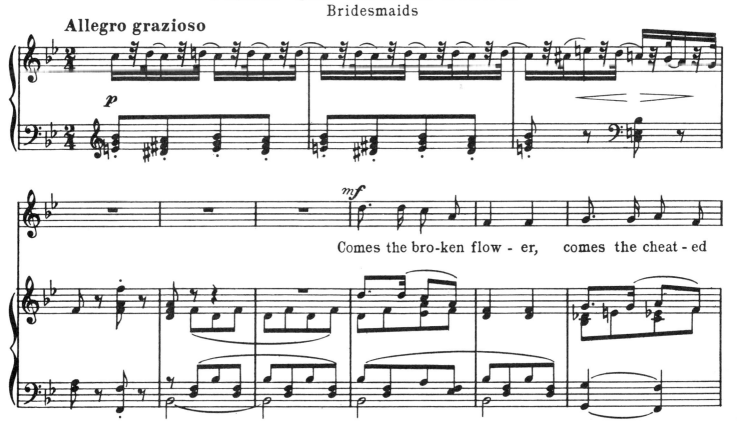

Comes the bro-ken flow - er, comes the cheat - ed

maid, Tho' the tem-pest low - er, rain and cloud will fade;

Take, O maid, the po - sies, tho' thy beau-ty rare, Shame the blush-ing

ro - ses, they are pass-ing fair, they___ are pass-ing fair.

Wear the_ flow - ers till they fade, hap - py, hap-py be thy

life, O maid! Wear the flow - ers till they fade,

Hap-py be thy life, O maid! Hap-py be thy life, O maid! Hap-py,_ hap-py be thy

life_ O maid!

The Judge is flirting with one of the bridesmaids and he sends a note to her by the Usher. She reads it rapt-urously and conceals it in the bosom of her dress. In the meantime Angelina announces that she is not really so very unhappy and she sings so sweetly that the Judge immediately transfers his affection to her. The Judge tells his associate that he has never seen so pretty a face and the Jurymen shake their fingers at him, calling him a "sly dog." However, when the Jury are asked how they like the lady, it develops that they are all madly in love with her also. The counsel for the plaintiff then addresses the Jury.

With A Sense Of Deep Emotion

The Counsel

Angelina has the entire sympathy of the Jury. She falls weeping on her attorney's shoulder and when led to the witness-box she starts fainting again. The Foreman of the Jury catches her in his arms and kisses her ardently. The Judge suggests that she do a little weeping on his shoulder too, so she staggers up to the bench and snuggles weeping on his shoulder. Everyone in the court-room is so moved that they shake their fists menacingly at Edwin. He endeavors to pacify them by suggesting that he marry Angelina today and his other girl to-morrow. The bridesmaids are all for Edwin, especially since he proposes to marry one girl to-day and another to-morrow. Even the Judge endorses this plan but Angelina's counsel refers to a law-book and states that in the Reign of James II a law was enacted that made it a serious crime to have more than one wife at a time. Now everyone agrees that this is indeed a serious dilemma, including Angelina and Edwin themselves.

I Love Him, I Love Him

Angelina and Edwin

1. I love him, I love him with smoke like a fur-nace. I'm

fer-vour un-ceas-ing, I wor-ship and mad-ly a-dore,
al-ways in li-quor, a ruf-fian, a bul-ly, a sot,

My blind a-do-ra-tion is
I'm sure I should thrash her, per-

ev-er in-creas-ing, My loss I shall ev-er de-plore.
haps I should kick her, I am such a ve-ry bad lot.

O__ see what a bless-ing, what
I'm__ not pre-po-sess-ing, as

love and ca-ress-ing, I've lost, and re-mem-ber it pray;
you may be guess-ing, she could-n't en-dure me a day;

When you I'm ad-dress-ing are
Re-call my pro-fess-ing when

Angelina clings to Edwin while he drags her all over the stage and finally throws her to the floor. The Judge tells the Jury that this case seems to concern liquor and as Edwin says he would treat her rough if he were tipsy, the only thing to do is to get him drunk and see just what he would do. Everyone strenuously objects to this method of settling the matter and so infuriates the Judge that he throws all the books and papers off his desk and settles the case in his own way.

Finale
All The Legal Furies Seize You

JUDGE

The ques-tion, gen-tle-men, is one of li-quor; You ask for guid-ance this is my re-ply; He says, when tip-sy, he would thrash and kick her, Let's make him tip-sy, gen-tle-men.

JUDGE

All the le-gal fu-ries seize you! No pro-po-sal seems to please you,

I can't sit up here all day, I must short-ly get a-way. Bar-ris-ters, and you, at-tor-neys,

Set out on your home-ward jour-neys; Gen - tle, sim-ple mind-ed ush-er, Get you,

if you like, to russ-ia; *RECIT.* Put your briefs up - on the

shelf, I will mar-ry her my-self.

This solution pleases everyone. The Judge and his bride dance the hornpipe on his desk. The Bridesmaids strew their flowers around the room and two huge Cupids descend from the wings. All join in the hilarity.

THE YEOMEN OF THE GUARD
or
The Merryman And His Maid

Libretto by
W. S. GILBERT

Music by
SIR ARTHUR SULLIVAN

Cast of Characters

SIR RICHARD CHOLMONDELEY . . . . . Lieutenant of the Tower
COLONEL FAIRFAX . . . . Under sentence of death
SERGEANT MERYLL . . . . A Yeoman of the Guard
LEONARD MERYLL . . . . His Son
JACK POINT . . . . A strolling Jester
WILFORD SHADBOLT . . . . The head jailer
PHOEBE MERYLL . . . . Meryll's daughter
ELSIE MAYNARD . . . . A strolling Singer
DAME CARRUTHERS . . . . House Keeper at the Tower
KATE . . . . Dame Carruther's niece

Scene — Tower of London.   Time — About 1500

Act I

Phoebe, Sergeant Meryll's daughter, is seated at her spinning wheel on the Green beneath the Tower of London, singing a sweet ballad.

When A Maiden Loves
Phoebe

1. When maid-en loves, she sits and sighs, She wan-ders to and
   maid-en loves, she mopes a-part, As owl mopes on a

fro; Un-bid-den tear-drops fill her eyes, And to all ques-tions she re-plies, With a
tree; Al-tho' she keen-ly feels the smart, She can-not tell what ails her heart, With it's

Shadbolt, who is in love with Phoebe, enters at the conclusion of her song. She bemoans the fact that Colonel Fairfax is to be executed for sorcery that very night. This makes Shadbolt extremely jealous. The Guard, commanded by Sergeant Meryll, is assembled and Dame Carruthers enters. Phoebe further declares that the Tower is a wicked place which has taken the lives of some of the finest and bravest men in England. This denunciation greatly displeases Dame Carruthers.

When Our Gallant Norman Foes

Dame Carruthers

Queen to save her head should come a-su-ing; There's a le-gend on its brow that is
con-science and for home in all its beau-ty; But the grim old fort-a-lice takes

el-o-quent to me, And it tells of du-ty done and du-ty do-ing. The
lit-tle heed of aught, That comes not in the mea-sure of its du-ty.

screw may twist and the rock may turn, And men may bleed and men may burn, On Lon-don town and

all its hoard, I keep my sol-emn watch and ward! The screw may twist, and the

rack may turn, And men may bleed and men may burn, On Lon-don town and all its horde I

keep my sol-emn watch and ward! watch and ward!

Sergeant Meryll and Phoebe are left alone on the stage. He tells her that he expects her brother Leonard to arrive from Windsor with a reprieve for Colonel Fairfax. Meryll is bound to help Fairfax because years before Fairfax had saved his life. They are doomed to be disappointed, however, for Leonard arrives without the reprieve. Meryll and Phoebe try to think of a way to save Fairfax. Leonard has been appointed a Yeoman of the Guard, for which reason he has returned to London. As the local officers do not yet know him, the three hit upon a plan to masquerade Fairfax as Meryll's son. Phoebe is to steal the keys from Shadbolt and Leonard is to lend his new uniform and disappear for a while. Colonel Fairfax is brought in under guard and Sir Richard Cholmondeley, Lieutenant of the Tower, and Sergeant Meryll both express their sympathy for him in his tragic predicament.

Is Life A Boon?
Colonel Fairfax

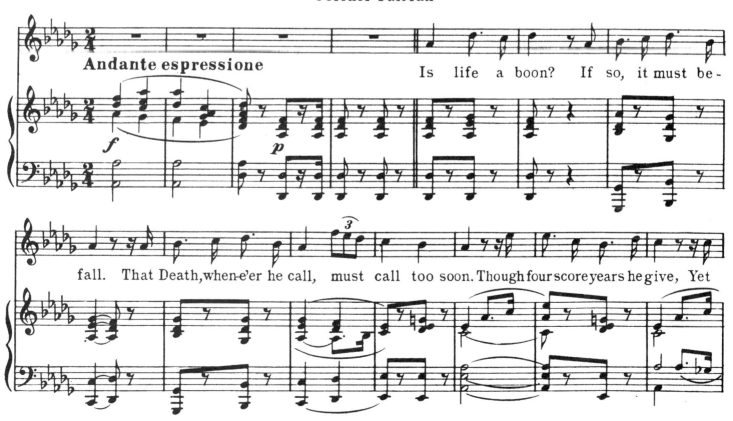

Is life a boon? If so, it must be-
fall. That Death, when-e'er he call, must call too soon. Though four score years he give, Yet

one would pray to live— An-oth-er moon! What kind of plaint have I, Who per-ish in Ju-

ly, Who per-ish in Ju - ly? I might have had to die, per-chance in June! I

might have had to die, per-chance in June!

Is life a thorn? Then count it not a whit! Nay count it not a whit! Man is well

done— with it. Soon as he's born He should all means es-say To put the

plague a - way; And I, war - worn, Poor cap - tured fu - gi-

tive, My life most glad-ly give. I might have had to live— An-oth - er morn! I

might have had to live, to live an-oth-er morn!

Fairfax tells them that he has been condemned through the machinations of a scheming relative, who will inherit his lands and fortune should he die a bachelor. Fairfax requests Cholmondeley to find him a woman, who will marry him for one hundred crowns and then be free again in a few hours, as he will be executed that night. This plan would also give Fairfax the satisfaction of thwarting the plans of his nefarious kinsman. Cholmondeley agrees to try to find such a woman. At this point Elsie Maynard and Jack Point enter followed by a crowd of peasants clamoring for them to make good their claim that they are singer and jester.

I Have A Song
Elsie and Point

193

sighed for the love of a la - dye, Heigh - dy! Heigh - dy!· Mis - er - y me,

lack - a - day - dee! He sipped no sup, and he craved no crumb, As he sighed for the love of a la-dye!

ELSIE   *POINT*

I have a song to sing, O! What is your song, O! _____

ELSIE

It is sung with the ring of the song maids sing who love with a love life-long, O! It's the

song of a mer-ry maid, peer-ly proud, Who lov'd a lord, and who laugh'd a-loud At the moan of a mer-ry man,

ELSIE   POINT   ELSIE

I have a song to sing, O! sing me your song, O! _____ It is sung with a sigh, and a

tear in the eye, For it tells of a right-ed wrong, O! It's a song of the mer-ry maid,

once so gay, Who turn'd on her heel and tripp'd a-way from the pea-cock pop-in-jay, brave-ly born, Who

turned up his no-ble nose with scorn At the hum-ble heart that he did not prize; So she

begged on her knees with down-cast eyes, For the love of the mer-ry man, mop-ing mum, Whose

soul was sad and whose glance was glum, Who sipp'd no sup, and who craved no crumb, As he

sighed for the love of a la - dye! Heigh-dy! Heigh-dy! Mis-er-y me, lack-a-day-dee! His

pains were o'er, and he sighed no more, For he lived in the love of a la - dye! Heigh-dy!

Heigh-dy! Mis-er-y me, lack-a-day-dee! His pains were o'er, and he sighed no more, For he

lived in the love of a la - dye!__

One of the rabble attempts to kiss Elsie, but she resists him with a dagger. The Lieutenant drives the crowd a-way and upon learning that Elsie and Point are not husband and wife, he offers her the opportunity of earning one hundred crowns by marrying Fairfax and being allowed to depart immediately after. She agrees, is blindfolded and led into the Tower and married to Fairfax. When she re-appears Shadbolt takes the bandage from her eyes.

Though Tear And Long-Drawn Sigh
Elsie

1. Tho' tear and long drawn sigh ill fit a bride,___ No sad-der wife than I the whole world wide! Ah, me! Ah, me! Yet maids there be who would con-sent to lose the ve-ry rose of youth The flow'r of

2. Ere half an hour has rung, a wid-ow I!___ Ah, heav'n he is too young, too brave to die! Ah, me! Ah, me! Yet wives there be so wea-ry worn, I trow, that they would scarce com-plain, So that they

According to their plans, Phoebe pretends to make ardent love to Shadbolt, steals the keys from him and keeps him interested until her father has freed Fairfax and returned the keys, which she successfully replaces in Shadbolt's belt. They leave the stage and Sergeant Meryll enters with Fairfax, disguised as a Yeoman of the Guard in Leonard's new uniform. He has shaved off his beard and mustache and is greeted by the Yeomen as Leonard, the son of Sergeant Meryll. The bell of St. Peter's church now begins to toll and the citizens enter. The headsman comes in and the block is placed in the center of the stage. Fairfax (as Leonard) and two other Yeomen are commanded to bring in the condemned prisoner.

Funeral March

Elsie is lamenting the fate of her newly-wedded husband whose face she has not even seen, when the Yeomen return in great excitement and announce that they found the cell door open and the prisoner gone. Cholmondeley orders Shadbolt's arrest holding him responsible for Fairfax's escape, and offers a thousand marks reward for his capture. Everyone hurries off to look for the escaped prisoner. Elsie faints in the arms of Fairfax, who does not even know that he is holding his own wife.

Act II

The second act is also on the Tower Green. It is moonlight. Several days have passed since the prisoner's escape. Dame Carruthers is upbraiding the wardens for their negligence. They admit that they are unable to find any trace whatever of Colonel Fairfax. Shadbolt enters with Jack Point, who has been established as Jester to the Lieutennant of the Tower. Shadbolt expresses the belief that Point has secured a very snug and easy post. Point vehemently disagrees with him.

A Private Buffoon
Jack Point

1. Oh! a pri-vate buf-foon is a light heart-ed loon, If you lis-ten to pop-u-lar
2. If your mas-ter is sur-ly, from get-ting up ear-ly, And tem-pers are short in the
3. Tho' your head it may rack with a bil-ious at-tack, And your sen-ses with tooth-ache you're

ru-mour; From the morn to the night he's so joy-ous and bright, And he
morn-ing; An in-op-por-tune joke is e-nough to pro-voke Him to
los-ing, Don't be mo-py and flat, they don't fine you for that, If you're

bub-bles with wit and good hu-mour! He's so quaint and so terse, both in prose and in verse, Yet though
give you at once a month's warn-ing! Then if you re-frain, he is at you a-gain, For he
pro-per-ly quaint and a - mus-ing! Tho' your wife ran a-way with a sol-dier that day, And took

peo-ple for-give his trans-gres-sion, There are one or two rules that all fam-i - ly fools, Must ob-
likes to get val-ue for mo-ney; He'll ask then and there, with an in-so-lent stare, If you
with her your tri-fle of mo-ney; Bless your heart, they don't mind they're ex-ceed-ing-ly kind, They don't

serve, if they love their pro-fes-sion! There are one or two rules, half a doz - en may - be, That all
know that you're paid to be fun-ny? It — adds to the task of a mer - ry-man's place, When your
blame you as long as you're fun-ny! It's a com-fort to feel, if your part-ner should flit, Tho' you

fam - i - ly fools, of what - ev - er de-gree,   Must ob-serve if they love their pro
prin - ci - pal asks, With a scowl on his face,   If you know that you're paid to be
suf-fer a deal, They don't mind it a bit,   They don't blame you so long as you're

Jack Point is in love with Elsie and his plans have all gone awry since the man she married is living and at large. It is the secret ambition of Shadbolt to be a Jester and the wily Point agrees to help him become one if Shadbolt will swear that he killed Fairfax as he was attempting to swim the moat. They leave, and Fairfax enters.   He is distressed over the fact that he has married a woman whom he has not even seen. Dame Carruthers enters with the startling news that she is sure Elsie is the woman who married Fairfax as she has overheard her talking in her sleep. Fairfax is interested but he cannot understand why a beautiful maid would marry a man doomed to be executed in a few hours.

Strange Adventure
Quartette

head-ed, in an hour on Tow-er Green!_____ Groom in drea-ry dun-geon
toll-ing, toll-ing, toll-ing, bim-a-boom!_____ Mod-est maid-en will not

ly-ing, Groom as good as dead or dy-ing, For a pret-ty maid-en sigh-ing, Pret-ty
tar-ry, Tho' but six-teen year she car-ry, She must mar-ry, she must mar-ry, Tho' the

maid of sev-en-teen! Sev-en, sev-en, sev-en-teen!
al-tar be a tomb, Tow-er, tow-er, tow-er tomb!

Tow-er

tomb!   Tow-er tomb! Tho' the al-tar be a tomb! Tow-er, tow-er, tow-er tomb!

Fairfax, as Leonard, makes love to Elsie and is delighted at her firm stand against his advances, proving that although she did not even know her husband, she regards as sacred the ties of marriage. A shot is heard and Cholmondeley and Sergeant Meryll rush in, followed by Point and Shadbolt. Shadbolt announces that he has killed Fairfax as he was swimming the moat. Point corroborates this story and tries to comfort Elsie by telling her that Fairfax was a brute, with hang-dog, ill-favored face at whom the Headsman himself would be frighened. He tries to make love to Elsie and renew his suit, but is so awkward about it that Fairfax undertakes to teach him the gentle art of wooing.

A Man Who Would Woo A Fair Maid

Fairfax and Elsie

man who would woo a fair maid,___ Should 'pren-tice him-self to the trade,___ And
made the best use of his time,___ His twig he'll so care-ful-ly lime,___ That

stu-dy all day in me-tho-di-cal way, How to flat-ter, ca-jole and per-suade! He should
ev-er-y bird will come down at his word, what-ev-er its plu-mage or clime! He must

'pren-tice him-self at four-teen, And prac-tice from mom-ing to e'en; And
learn that the thrill of a touch, May mean lit-tle, or noth-ing or much; It's an

when he's of age, if he will, I'll en - gage, he may cap-ture the heart of a Queen, the heart
in - stru-ment rare, to be han-dled with care, And ought to be treat - ed as such, Ought

of a Queen!
to be treat-ed as such!   It is pure - ly a mat-ter of skill, which

all may at-tain if they will,   But ev - er - y Jack, he must stu-dy the knack, If he

wants to make sure of his Jill   If he wants to make sure___ of his

Jill.   If he's Jill.

Fairfax thereupon proceeds to make love to Elsie so ardently that Point is extremely annoyed. Phoebe is also distressed as she thinks he is just trifling with Elsie. This in turn makes Shadbolt jealous and Phoebe agrees to marry him to pacify him. The real Leonard returns at this point with the glad tidings that Fairfax's reprieve, which had been withheld by the scheming kinsman, was signed by the King and delivered to the Lieutenant of the Tower. The delighted Fairfax reveals his identity to Elsie and they happily embrace while Phoebe reconciles herself to Shadbolt. Dame Carruthers, who has been slyly flirting with Sergeant Meryll for years, now openly declares her love and the opera ends happily for all, except perhaps Jack Point who is the only one left out in the cold.

Finale
Entire Company

glance was glum, Who sipp'd no sup, and who craved no crumb, As he sighed for the love of a

la - dye! Heigh - dy! Heigh - dy! Mis - er - y me, lack - a - day - dee! He

sipp'd no sup and he craved no crumb, As he sighed for the love of a la - dye! Heigh - dy!

Heigh - dy! Mis - er - y me, lack - a - day dee! He sipp'd no sup and he craved no crumb, As he

sighed for the love of a la - dye!